He Stopped Loving Her Today

HE STOPPED LOVING HER TODAY

GEORGE JONES, BILLY SHERRILL, AND THE PRETTY-MUCH TOTALLY TRUE STORY OF THE MAKING OF THE GREATEST COUNTRY RECORD OF ALL TIME

JACK ISENHOUR

UNIVERSITY PRESS OF MISSISSIPPI / JACKSON

American Made Music Series

David Evans, General Editor	John Edward Hasse
Barry Jean Ancelet	Kip Lornell
Edward A. Berlin	Bill Malone
Joyce J. Bolden	Eddie S. Meadows
Rob Bowman	Manuel H. Peña
Susan C. Cook	David Sanjek
Curtis Ellison	Wayne D. Shirley
William Ferris	Robert Walser

www.upress.state.ms.us

The University Press of Mississippi is a member of
the Association of American University Presses.

First printing 2011
∞
Library of Congress Cataloging-in-Publication Data

Isenhour, Jack.
He stopped loving her today : George Jones, Billy Sherrill, and the pretty-much totally true story of the making
of the greatest country record of all time / Jack Isenhour.
p. cm. — (American made music series)
Includes bibliographical references and index.
ISBN 978-1-61703-101-4 (cloth : alk. paper) — ISBN
978-1-61703-102-1 (ebook) 1. Country music—History
and criticism. 2. Country music—Production and direction—History. 3. Jones, George, 1931– 4. Sherrill, Billy.
I. Title.
ML3524.I84 2011
781.64209—dc22   2011004411

British Library Cataloging-in-Publication Data available

For Dana

CONTENTS

ACKNOWLEDGMENTS

Thanks to Joan Barnfield, who served time at the original Possum Holler; Connie Woods and Glynn and Brenda Dowdle, who knew somebody who knew somebody; Judge-John-Brown for the goat roast and backstage passes; and Sheriff Daron Hall who took us along for the ride.

Thanks to "He Stopped Loving Her Today" co-writer Bobby Braddock and A Team/"He Stopped Loving Her Today" bass player Bob Moore and wife Kitra who were beyond generous with their time and insight.

Thanks to Alison Booth at Sony, who, at Bobby Braddock's request, searched the CBS/Epic archives from Nashville to New York. Thanks to Billy Sherrill and daughter Cathy Lale for the rare interview, and to fellow talkers "He Stopped Loving Her Today" co-songwriter Curly Putman and "He Stopped Loving Her Today" session musicians Charlie McCoy, Hargus "Pig" Robbins, Jerry Carrigan, and Pete Wade; engineers Lou Bradley and Ron "Snake" Reynolds; and background singer Millie Kirkham.

Thanks to then Bandit Records executives Evelyn Shriver and Susan Nadler; Musicians' Hall of Fame creator Joe Chambers, back-in-the-day, Kenny-Rogers' producer Larry Butler, and Billy Sherrill's "gal Friday" turned label executive Emily Mitchell.

Thanks to music scholars Joli Jensen (who read an early manuscript), the late Richard Peterson for his myth-shattering book *Creating Country Music: Fabricating Authenticity*, Paul Kingsbury, Nick Tosches, Charles Wolfe, Bill Ivey, Bill C. Malone, Nicholas Dawidoff, Douglas B. Green, Patrick Carr, Craig Havighurst, Dianne Pecknold, Marc Fisher, Randy Rudder, and to Reference Librarian Dawn Oberg at the Country Music Hall of Fame and Museum and Nashville Room photo guru Beth Odle at the Nashville Public Library.

Thanks to George Jones biographers Bob Allen, Dolly Carlisle, Tom Carter, and Jim Brown; *Billboard* chart compiler Joel Whitburn; and journalists Michael Kosser, Phillip Self, Rick Bolsom, Robert Oermann, Beverly Keel, and a cast of thousands at the *Nashville Banner* and the *Tennessean*.

I am indebted to them all. And finally, thanks most of all to my wife and partner Dana E. Moore. None of this gets written without Dana. Not a word.

He Stopped Loving Her Today

PROLOGUE
Shattering Glass in a Minor Key

First, get your heart broke. Bad. By the love of your life. Those felled by teenage crushes need not apply. Second, light one up for the first time in years and sip something aged in small batches in a barrel all its own. Finally, come midnight, any midnight, listen, rinse, repeat to "He Stopped Loving Her Today." Moan with the steel. Study the lyrics. There will be a quiz. As for cheating, that will be encouraged. Just don't count on anybody taking your sorry ass back.

He Stopped Loving Her Today

He said I'll love you 'til I die.
She told him you'll forget in time.
As the years went slowly by,
She still preyed upon his mind.

He kept her picture on his wall.
Went half crazy now and then.
He still loved her through it all,
Hoping she'd come back again.

Kept some letters by his bed
Dated nineteen-sixty-two.
He had underlined in red
Every single "I love you."

I went to see him just today,
Oh but I didn't see no tears.

3

All dressed up to go away.
First time I'd seen him smile in years.

(chorus)
He stopped loving her today.
They placed a wreath upon his door.
And soon they'll carry him away.
He stopped loving her today.

(spoken)
You know she came to see him one last time.
Oh and we all wondered if she would.
And it kept running through my mind,
This time he's over her for good.

(chorus)
He stopped loving her today.
They placed a wreath upon his door.
And soon they'll carry him away.
He stopped loving her today.

I had put it off for a couple of weeks. Bought the latest George Jones CD at Tower (R.I.P.), threw it into the rubble on my desk, and acted like I forgot about it. But I always knew it was there waiting. Lurking. So the time came and I dug it out of the pile, out from under a copy of the *Sporting News*, an invoice from cigaretteexpress.com—thirty-six dollars and change for one lousy carton (I've since quit)—and a review of the CD from livedaily.com.

"In superb voice," it read.

The CD, called *Hits I Missed . . . And One I Didn't*, was a compilation of one man's failures, said the ballyhoo, songs that got away, standards even, that George Jones, a guy who was supposed to be a "song man," turned down.

"George Jones could smell a hit plum across town," recalled former Starday label promoter Gabe Tucker.

Maybe so, but, according to the hype, George didn't pick up the scent on the first eleven songs on the CD: classics like "Funny How Time Slips Away" and "Detroit City." Whatever. In this collection, it was the song Jones didn't pass over that I was interested in: a remake of "He Stopped Loving Her Today."

For months I'd been doing research for a book about "He Stopped Loving Her Today," the 1980 smash hit that saved George Jones's career, if not his life. I'd been listening to the song over and over, talking to the studio musicians, the background singers, the engineers, the songwriters, and legendary producer Billy Sherrill. You remember Billy, he's the Country Music Hall of Famer from Phil Campbell, Alabama, who discovered Tammy Wynette and Tanya Tucker, made Charlie Rich a star, cowrote "Stand By Your Man" and "Almost Persuaded," and, for more than twenty years, was a hit-making machine for Columbia/Epic, where he was a producer and songwriter, not to mention Nashville label chief.

"As my grandfather used to say, I was 'the man with the fuzzy balls,'" said Sherrill.

That Billy Sherrill.

I was talking to Billy and the rest trying to learn everything there was to know about the making of the best country record-ing of all time. In the middle of all this yakking about the past, I got a call out of the blue and was sidetracked for the summer co-writing the Dennis Rodman memoir, *I Should Be Dead By Now*. When I came up for air, I got the news: while I was distracted, George and producer Keith Stegall had recorded a remake of "He Stopped Loving Her Today."

This new version of the classic song could have presented a problem. What if George did it better? What if there were a new best recording of all time? Would I have to start over?

I knew the recording should be better. In the late seventies, early eighties, when Billy Sherrill was wringing the original "He Stopped Loving Her Today" out of a worse-for-wear George Jones one note at a time, the singer was at the low point of his life. Still heartbroken over Tammy, snorting coke when he wasn't guzzling bourbon, at times homeless, bankrupt, George Jones was in the checkout lane. Friends and fans were left wondering not if, but when they would be following Jones's miles-long funeral proces-sion out Nashville's Thompson Lane to Woodlawn Cemetery and what the headline would read. Car wreck? Overdose? Liver dis-ease? Heart attack? Pure orneriness?

"He was withering away and was killing himself," said Sherrill. "He got down to way under a hundred pounds."

In 1979 George Jones was a dead man walking. On the rare occasions when he showed up at Billy's office sane and sober enough to actually be coaxed into the studio to work, he was hoarse from snorting coke. That pissed Sherrill off. But there was none of the righteous indignation you might expect from this son of a Baptist preacher. Instead, Billy went for a qualified "Just say 'yes.'"

"If you gotta be a druggie," Sherrill recalled telling Jones, "do like Ray Charles did. Get on heroin. Don't use the only drug that rots your vocal chords."

When Jones finally got to the point where Sherrill could roll tape on "He Stopped Loving Her Today," George screwed up the tune. Remember that Kris Kristofferson song "Help Me Make It Through the Night"?

> Take the ribbon from your hair,
> Shake it loose and let it fall.

"I was singing it with that tune," said George.

"Drove me insane," said Sherrill.

Later, after George got the tune straight, he had trouble reading the spoken verse. Seems George could sing well enough when he was drunk, but he couldn't speak without slurring his words.

That's the kind of foolishness Billy Sherrill had to put up with while producing the original version of "He Stopped Loving Her Today." So I was thinking a generation later, there was a real chance the refitted, booze- and coke-free George Jones, with a little help from today's digital technology that can "tune" a singing waiter into respectability, could sound even better on this new version of the classic. But I hoped not. And not just because I didn't want to start over. It was way more than that.

Don't we all secretly like the idea of this crazed, suffering son of a bitch singing his heart out, giving voice to our pain? In the original, George sounds like what we have all felt like when "the-one-they-write-the-books-about" leaves us (all men are pond scum, women are no damn good) and we're left alone in that dark house wallowing in it, hoping, with the help of one last short one, to become reacquainted with our long lost friend, sleep. So the idea of today's clean-living, model-citizen George Jones singing "He Stopped Loving Her Today" on a Thursday morning at some Nashville studio and then dropping by the Sylvan Park Cafe on the way home for a meat-and-three and a slice of the restaurant's famous chocolate meringue pie before patting his pot gut and heading on back to Franklin fat and happy in a black BMW sedan, license plate NOSHOWII, to hang out on that little sissy farm of his—well, it just ain't right. When George Jones sings we want to hear a pistol cocking, wheels spinning in a gravel honky tonk parking lot, slamming doors, and a clinched-teeth, bitter hissing of "I'll kick that sum-bitch's ass!" The real George Jones, vintage George Jones, is not the sound of a purring engine of a German luxury sedan cruising down I-65 to the suburbs, but of shattering glass in a minor key. So the real question with this new version of "He Stopped Loving Her Today" was whether a man who was no longer "singing his life" could still pull it off; whether a healthy, happy, pain-free George Jones could do justice to the greatest country song of all time—after the fact. After the booze. After the cocaine. After the heartbreak. Only one way to find out.

· · ·

I had a plan. I would listen to the original recording of "He Stopped Loving Her Today" one last time. Get reacquainted with this tale of a man who has to die to get over a woman. Then, done with the original, I'd pop in the new CD, skip past the first eleven songs so I could hear version one and version two of the best country song of all time back-to-back. It was exactly 4:02 on a Tuesday afternoon. Going cold turkey. No booze. No heartbreak in sight. Just another day at the office.

I listened to the new version. Once. Twice. Three times. Something wasn't right. The Charlie McCoy harmonica was gone. The Jordanaires—the backup singers—were gone. The woodblock was gone, replaced by barely audible rim shots. The strings were gone. Pianist Pig Robbins, the only musician to play on both versions, had a bigger part to play. In the original I couldn't hear him until the mournful lick at the very end although Billy Sherrill says he was probably playing all way through, just mixed way under. In the update, Pig played where the harmonica came in on the original and the steel guitar filled in for the strings. The song started and ended exactly the same—George's a cappella open and Pig's closing lick—but it felt more tentative, loose, lacking that feeling of a locomotive headed down the track: the relentless, stubborn, not-gonna-let-you-off-the-hook inevitability, the single-minded "lean" of the original. Billy Sherrill's a-place-for-every-note-and-every-note-in-its-place production style was gone and what was left was a sense the song might jump the tracks at any moment. As for George, in contrast to the original, he sounded kind of wooden, like he was reading the lyrics. Lord knows that's a possibility. The man has been known to mangle a line or two in concert. But don't blame it on age.

"He's always missed words and had a hard time," said Sherrill.

• • •

Days later I came back to the new cut again. I had figured out what was missing. Big picture: the Nashville Sound. The Owen Bradley, Anita Kerr, Chet Atkins prettifying of country music that took hold in the late fifties to the dismay of hard-core fans everywhere.

In the "Chet Atkins compromise," as some critics called it, producers did away with the fiddles and steel guitar, established unholy alliances with the Jordanaires and the Anita Kerr Singers, and then took it one step further by adding moonlighting violinists from the Nashville Symphony. Voilà! The Nashville Sound.

"We took the twang out of it, Owen Bradley and I," Atkins told writer Nicolas Dawidoff.

All this in hopes of making "country" records that would sell to mainstream, pop audiences. For purists, the Nashville Sound was blasphemy, baby, sweet-and-sour pork in a pit-barbeque world. They hated the "mooing vocal choruses" and "violins from hell," saw this softening of the country sound as a betrayal of the highest order.

Still, the Nashville Sound had staying power. And twenty years later when the original "He Stopped Loving Her Today" was being cut, the strings and background singers were still around and Sherrill had, as Jones biographer Bob Allen poetically put it, "picked up the bouncing ball that had been kicked in motion by pioneering Nashville Sound producers Chet Atkins and Owen Bradley."

But there was good news for purists: the steel guitar was back in, center stage even. This cross-breeding of styles (some call it "Countrypolitan") is what we hear on the original cut of "He Stopped Loving Her Today." So the Nashville Sound–free remake on *Hits I Missed* isn't really an updated version of the song. Stylistically it's more like a 1948, honky-tonk version, the version Jones does in concert—no violins, no Jordanaires, no foolin'—at, say, the Ryman Auditorium, the "Mother Church of Country Music," on a lovely spring night. That's about as good as it's gonna get. Magic. And on that particular evening I was going to hear it happen if the Judge made good on his promise of tickets.

Oh, and as for the burning question: will the stripped-down, more country version of "He Stopped Loving Her Today" on the *Hits I Missed* album make anybody forget the 1980 original?

Be serious.

PART ONE
GEORGE JONES
LIVE

1

VACANT, INERT CIPHER

Saturday, downtown Nashville. The early arrivals, packed cheek to jowl, flowed downhill on the sidewalks flanking the Ryman Auditorium. On the Fifth Avenue side, the crowd split as it neared the auditorium, the George Jones fans peeling off to the left and the sports fans continuing on down toward the arena. The temperature was in the sixties and the forecast rain, but after a day of sunshine there wasn't an umbrella in sight. Over on Fourth Avenue, a scalper moved up the slope against the grain, one baby step at a time, holding a small sign above his head: I NEED TICKETS PLEASE.

At the Ryman's east entrance dozens of fans milled around while others, mostly seniors, sat on the low brick walls surrounding the courtyard, some at the feet of a statue of Captain Tom Ryman, the building's namesake. The hard-drinking riverboat captain had built what was first a religious meeting house after he was "saved" by a Bible-thumping evangelist in 1885.

Seeing the statue, it was obvious we should've planned our rendezvous at this landmark. Instead, my wife Dana Moore and Judge-John-Brown (it's always one word: "Judge-John-Brown;" never just "Judge" or "Judge Brown") had decided we would meet at George Jones's tour bus to pick up backstage passes. Turned out there were three identical purple and silver buses in the Jones entourage, all unmarked.

Back when George was a pup, a bus with your name plastered all over it, a rolling billboard, was a coming-of-age status symbol for a country singer. No more. Now there are too many crazies out there to offer yourself up as a clay pigeon in the skeet shoot of life, so to speak. Not that it was that hard to figure out which of the three buses belonged to George. The line of twenty-five or so autograph seekers was a dead giveaway, as people handed this and that through the bus door for George to sign.

That was at the bus on the far left. The next bus over belonged to the band. Then came a white RV carrying the band's instruments where they had made up for the lack of labeling on the buses by stenciling "George Jones Concert Tour" in big letters on the side. The last bus was for "Barry and Sheri": that's Barry Smith and Sheri Copland, the husband and wife act that would share the stage with George. Think Donnie and Marie with about half the teeth.

A forty-something couple in matching western-detailed red shirts and black cowboy hats asked me to take their picture in front of George's black BMW. George drove and his wife Nancy rode, the guy assured me. He said to make sure I got the NOSHOW2 vanity plate in the picture. Done.

Still no Judge-John-Brown.

•   •   •

The George Jones "He-Stopped-Loving-Her-Today" project had officially begun about a year before when the white limo rented for the occasion rolled up the driveway of Jones's Franklin, Tennessee home. On board, Dana's old friend, Davidson County sheriff Daron Hall and his wife Ginger, Dana and me, and a visiting sheriff from North Carolina with his family. The visiting sheriff was in town for a meeting of the National Sheriffs' Association and he had called ahead asking for an audience with Jones. That's like a tourist in Rome asking to do brunch with the Pope, but Daron managed to pull it off. Then Daron made the mistake of mentioning this to Dana and me. So here we all were on George Jones's doorstep, soon to get an up close and personal view of the legend himself.

We were met by a third sheriff, this one from Williamson County, who ushered us inside. Soon we were all standing around in the living room of "the greatest country singer of all time."

Unreal.

George showed up and it was clear he didn't know who we were or why we were there. Whatever. After more than fifty years in show business, he had marched to this tune before and soon the pictures were being taken and the autographs being signed.

Neat as a pin, every strand of white hair perfectly placed, George wore starched, ironed jeans; a crisp, short-sleeved shirt with a red and blue windowpane plaid; and rose-tinted glasses. George had been wearing those glasses ever since his self-described "beady brown eyes" led a couple of deejays to nickname him "Possum" back in the days of the coal-fired pedal steel.

Later, George, who's seen the inside of a jail or two, ended up posing with three high sheriffs at once. When somebody pointed that out, he faked a flinch and eyed the nearest exit. That's about as animated as the man got.

Some stars handle these "meet and greets" differently. Like Dolly Parton. From the moment she enters a room, she's in total control. Chatting nonstop, she poses for pictures, autographs whatever is put under her nose, and spends time with everybody while at the same time keeping it moving. (I know this because Dana worked for Dolly for a couple of years.) George, on the other hand, doesn't act, he reacts. Dolly's active. He's passive. She's an extrovert. He's shy by nature. This passivity has led some folks to misread him.

A decade or so back, writer Nick Tosches described George as "vacant," as "a man whose unequivocal soulfulness abided incongruously beneath an inert mind."

"Without a song," wrote Tosches, "he was a cipher."

So Tosches all but called the man a moron. Admittedly, George Jones is not the most articulate guy in the world. What's more, in public, he's not the least bit philosophical about his life or his music, and he once described himself to the *Village Voice* as "just an ignorant country boy who never had much schoolin." But vacant, inert, a cipher? That's cold. Consider the source. Nick Tosches was born in Newark, New Jersey, and didn't have the benefit of growing up in the small town South where you can always find a couple of characters like George Jones hanging around.

"What I like most about George is that when you meet him, he is just like some ole guy that works down at the gas station," said Alan Jackson.

Exactly. "Nondescript" is too gaudy a word for George Jones. The man is as plain as an unbuttered biscuit. Then he opens his mouth to sing and it's apparent that the difference between George and all those vacant, inert ciphers sitting on benches in the courthouse square whittling points on the ends of sticks is that God, in his infinite wisdom, loaded up George Jones with all the talent. He's better at what he does than anybody else. Ever. That's not me talking. It's the opinion of people like Johnny Cash, Waylon Jennings, Garth Brooks, and Tom T. Hall.

"I've never talked to a country music person whose favorite singer wasn't George Jones," said Hall.

Even Frank Sinatra once called George "the second best male singer in America." A *Time* magazine critic took it even further, calling Jones "*the* greatest American popular singer of the twentieth century." But however he is ranked, everybody agrees there's nothing vacant, inert, or cipherish about George Jones's talent. Meanwhile the rest of us are left wondering, "Why him and not me?" Why exactly did God give all the talent to Jones, this alcoholic grade school dropout, this person of lesser virtue, when all of us happy white Christian Rotarians were ready and willing to bear the burden? Well, now, that will just have to remain one of the mysteries.

•   •   •

The seed was planted when the out-of-town sheriff handed George a hardback copy of *I Lived to Tell It All*, the singer's autobiography. While signing the book, George said he wished the publisher had included more stuff about the music.

"Nobody has ever done a book about the music," he said.

In the made-for-TV movie, I'll leap forward right then and say, "George, I'll write that book and we'll sell a million of 'em!"

Didn't happen.

I was slow on my feet and it would be months before I did the research and found out George was right. The three George Jones biographies are more about drinking and drugging than picking and singing. Same goes for George's autobiography, a book that critic Nicholas Dawidoff called "a massive chronicle of

vile behavior related with brutal candor" in which "next to nothing revealing is said about the art of singing."

So I made a call here and a call there, decided to focus on
"He Stopped Loving Her Today," got George's blessing, and soon
began writing a book "about the music." Then there was a happy
accident. In the midst of learning pretty much everything anybody would ever need to know about the making of "He Stopped
Loving Her Today," I found out pretty much everything a fan
needs to know about country music. The gist? Well, as you'll see
throughout the rest of this tome, you can't believe everything
you read in the popular media. So put aside all those fan-mag
assumptions and get ready for a bumpy ride.

• • •

Judge-John-Brown finally showed up at the Ryman. He was running late after having spent the previous evening at a Willie Nelson concert in Tunica, Mississippi, about five hours south. His
driver didn't get him home until 2:45 in the morning.

Judge-John-Brown stood out in this crowd, looking natty
in his hunter green blazer; light blue Oxford cloth shirt; khaki
pants; and maroon and white bowtie. He was in his sixties, bald
on top with a white beard and moustache; wore thick, wire-
rimmed glasses; and, like most of us, could stand to lose a few
pounds. While he may not have looked the part, Judge-John-
Brown probably was the biggest country fan there. This was his
seventy-somethingth time to see George Jones and he has been
to over six hundred Willie Nelson concerts.

The judge pulled out an "All Access" pass that he had figured
would get me, at least, backstage. But there was a major hitch.
The pass was from the previous year and nobody would honor
it. He knew this because George's manager already had tried an
identical pass at the stage door.

"He said, 'I'm Reggie Mac. I'm his manager,'" said Judge
Brown. "And the guy says, 'I don't care who you are, you can't get
in without a pass.'"

Judge-John-Brown has an Old South drawl thick as chilled
molasses. When he says "am" it comes out "a.m." It's an accent so

thick even southerners take notice; so exaggerated that an actor using it—maybe playing Big Daddy in *Cat on a Hot Tin Roof*—would be accused of stooping to caricature. So how does Judge Brown describe his accent?

"Nashville," he said.

Maybe so, but I've been in town over twenty-five years and I've never heard anything like it.

"Who else in town talks like that?" I asked.

"I dunno," said the Judge. "Y'know, most of them talk wrong, I guess." He smiles. "It's just sort of southern, slow. And I'm always surprised when I hear myself."

It's people like the Judge who can really throw you when you're trying to describe a typical country music fan. He's as southern as pecan pie, but he's also a lawyer, a pharmacist (the family business), and the stepfather of a onetime captain of the Dartmouth football team.

Some critics still cling to the notion that country fans are from the southern working class. Others talk about hillbillies, rednecks, trailer trash. But the idea that most country fans come from the underbelly of society has long been wrong.

A survey cited in the *New York Times* in 2003 showed that, in the New York market, country radio listeners were all but identical to those of leading adult contemporary stations. The difference? Country music fans tended to be "a little more affluent," and were more likely to have "managerial" jobs.

I checked out the fans in line at the Ryman. There was a teenaged boy, maybe sixteen, still with a little baby fat, wearing a brown T-shirt that read "Save a tree, harvest a buck." So add flabby, teenage, deer hunters to the list and NASCAR fans. Dana spotted three men in Dale Earnhardt Jr. T-shirts. Then there were all the seniors: keepers of the Roy Acuff–Hank Williams, hillbilly honky-tonk flame, I suspect. Off to the side, a very tall, war-prisoner-thin man channeled Hank in his brown, western cut leather jacket, cowboy hat, and boot-leg jeans. Later I would see a Chinese guy and a bespectacled, forty-something preppy in a blue blazer and khakis. All country music fans. It's going to take a lot of fence to corral all these folks. Maybe Bill Ivey can help.

Back when Ivey headed the Country Music Foundation, the scholarly arm of the Country Music Hall of Fame, he came up with what he called an "industry" definition of country music. Country music, wrote Ivey, is "records that country radio will play and that country fans will buy." Following that same train of thought, a Bill Ivey country fan might be anybody that listens to country radio, buys country recordings, and attends country concerts. That'll fence in our deer-hunting teenager, both Presidents Bush, Judge-John-Brown, poor white trash, and the urbane Ivey himself, who served some time as the Chairman of the National Endowment for the Arts.

For the time being, forget that the beauty (and the ugly) of the Ivey approach is that these definitions can be applied without ever once talking about the music itself. (This is helpful in a category of music whose charts have at one time or another laid claim to both Hank Williams and Engelbert Humperdinck.)

One more thing.

Card-carrying country fans are not like pop music fans. It goes much deeper. Country fans "define themselves in and through the music," seeing themselves as outsiders versus the mainstream, observed country music scholar Joli Jensen. Vanderbilt's Richard Peterson took it a step further. "Identification with country music today is like identification with an ethnic group," he wrote. And with that comes an "associated way of life," and an "imagined place in society." Like other ethnicities, membership is not predicated on money or class. So there's room in the country corral not only for waitresses, truck drivers, and farmers—the working class—but also for all the professors, lawyers, doctors, and CEOs who in the privacy of their own home—"Pull down the shades, Adelaide!"—prefer a fiddle to a violin.

2

ART AND MONEY

Judge-John-Brown reappeared with a fist full of "All Access" passes. They were about half-again as big as a credit card, laminated to last, and had a color picture of George on the front. With these babies we would be able to roam around the Ryman Auditorium at will and, if anybody asked, could answer with that line we'd been waiting a lifetime to deliver: "I'm with the band."

"I have to have these back," said Judge-John-Brown as we looped the passes around our necks.

We made our way to the alley running down the south side of the Ryman. Like most alleys, it was not inviting. We passed a line of grubby, oversized, plastic garbage cans as Judge Brown stuffed something in his ears. I jumped in with some small talk about earplugs and how annoyingly loud the music can get even at country concerts.

Oops.

"I've completely lost my hearing in one ear," said Judge-John-Brown, not the least bit offended, and it was only then I spotted the amber-colored, coiled plastic tube winding its way into his ear.

The tourist haunts that front what the locals call Lower Broadway have rear entrances which open into the Ryman alley. We passed the back door of a honky tonk called the Stage, then Jack's BBQ, where the smell of smoked pork wafted over a small, uninviting patio with three or four tables. Soon we heard bluegrass spilling out the back door of "the world famous" Tootsie's Orchid Lounge, once the Opry's unofficial watering hole.

From the alley we could see over Tootsie's to the sports arena and the decorative spire out front that's meant to look like the old WSM radio antenna. There's another WSM-like "antenna" perched on top of the Country Music Hall of Fame a block away. These nods to Nashville's WSM are appropriate. The creative, technical, and business people who at one time or another worked at WSM, whether for the station, the Grand Ole Opry, or both, pretty much built Music City U.S.A. People like Fred Rose, who discovered and mentored Hank Williams; Patsy Cline's producer Owen Bradley, who started out as a staff pianist at the station; Carl Jenkins and Aaron Shelton, the two WSM engineers who founded Castle Studios, Nashville's first commercial recording studio; Opry announcer Jim Bulleit, the man behind Bullet Records, an early Nashville label; and Jack Stapp, a onetime Opry GM who along with Buddy Killen turned Tree Publishing into a music industry powerhouse.

Most historians put a happy face on all this, but as Michael Kosser reports in *How Nashville Became Music City U.S.A.*, by the mid-fifties moonlighting had become such a problem at WSM that the president of the company issued an ultimatum: them or me. When forced to choose between the radio station and their outside interests, some like the boys at Castle came home to Mama, reported Kosser, while others like Opry house manager Jim Denny ignored the threat and were eventually fired. Denny landed on his feet, establishing something called Cedarwood Publishing. Today this family squabble is all but forgotten as WSM is given its due in the local architecture.

Judge-John-Brown led us up the short flight of concrete steps to the Ryman stage door, where a short, uniformed guard with a very gray, very flat flattop haircut, circa George Jones 1962, checked out our passes and waved us in. That easy. No metal detector. No shoe removal. No pat-down. We stepped into a long narrow hallway made narrower still by equipment cases stacked against the walls. There were maybe two dozen people wandering around: staff, visitors, hangers-on like us. To the left about twenty paces was the stage. To the right, around the corner another twenty paces, was a closed door that opened into the back of the auditorium.

George's wife Nancy cruised by. "My sweet, baby, darlin', Judge Brown," she cooed, never even slowing down.

There were framed black-and-white photos on the beige wall: a young Bill Monroe, an even younger George Jones, Marty

Robbins, Elvis, and Tony Bennett—all people who had stood where we were standing. Tony Bennett made the cut because he was one of the first pop singers to score a pop hit with a country song, taking Hank Williams's "Cold Cold Heart" to number one in 1951. Not pictured: Will Rogers, Enrico Caruso, W. C. Fields, Tallulah Bankhead, and Eleanor Roosevelt, who had done their time backstage at the Ryman.

George sneaked up the back stairs and into a dressing room marked "Private, Nancy Jones." Earlier, Sheri of "Barry and Sheri" had announced from the stage that members of the George Jones Fan Club could get autographs if they came to the door at the back of the auditorium. Soon George came out of the dressing room, the ear monitors he wore to hear on stage dangling out of his ears. He set up shop in the corridor just inside the auditorium door. The fans came and went, the pace quick, but not frantic. Nancy managed all this, introducing folks, sometimes even taking pictures.

I stood six or seven steps to George's left watching. This fan club bunch was skewing younger than the fans outside, I thought, as two beaming sisters, maybe thirteen and fifteen, posed with George followed by a forty-something woman in black T-shirt with "George Jones" stenciled on the front in white. Then came another forty-something woman, this one with a wild-ass, curly blond pony tail, hair going every-which-a-way.

As I stood watching, I was thinking that the "All-Access," I'm-with-the-band, backstage pass that put me here was really cool. I would keep on thinking that right up until the moment George took the stage and the Jones Boys hit the first notes of "Why Baby Why?," George's first charted record back in 1955. It was then I realized all I could hear was a garbled wall of noise. The sound system was geared for the people out front, of course, not the people standing in the wings. And while I could tell George was singing "Why Baby Why?" a bit slower than the original recording, that was about it. Then there was all the yapping going on. Instead of listening to the show, the people backstage were trying to talk over the music like it was Muzak.

I had forgotten "Out front is the place to be, out where the illusions are," as Patrick Anderson put it in the *New York Times* thirty years ago. Thanks to my pass, I would be able to tell my grandchildren that George Jones patted me on the back on his way on stage at the, by-God, Ryman Auditorium. What I wouldn't be able to tell them was what he sounded like once he got there. So it was time to reposition my insider self somewhere I could actually hear what was going on.

The applause died down after "Once You've Had the Best," a 1973 hit, and George delivered his usual line—"Keep that up and I'm liable to stay here to three or four o'clock in the morning"— and got the usual cheer. He then launched into "The Race Is On," another one of those upper register, up-tempo tunes that marked his career before the coming of Billy Sherrill.

I ducked out the side door where the autograph seekers had come in and stood in darkness for a moment getting my bearings. I was at the very back of the auditorium, far left, and could only see George in profile. I moved around to the center to get a better look as he kicked off "Choices," the 1999 hit that won him the Grammy and put him back on the country charts for the first time in almost two years.

Standing at the back of the auditorium, I could barely see the top of George's head because of the low-hanging balcony, and, without stooping, couldn't see the onstage video projections at all. I blamed the bad sightlines on lousy design, thinking the balcony—the so-called "Confederate Gallery," which had been added five years after the auditorium was built in 1885—was some kind of on-second-thought, jury-rigged deal. Wrong. It was in the original plans, but got cut to save money and was reincarnated about a decade later to meet the needs of the Tennessee Centennial Celebration. The Confederate Veterans Association got naming rights by paying for it.

I tucked my palm-sized tape recorder under my notepad hiding the glowing red record light from the ushers. NO CAMERAS/AUDIO/VIDEO, the tickets plainly read, but the recorder was a tool that kept me from having to constantly take notes about everything that was said, like when Barry started selling a three-CD set of George's greatest hits from the stage.

"Fifty songs starting in 1955 with 'Why Baby Why,'" Barry announced. "Not just something somebody threw together, these are the actual cuts starting in 1955 and going all way up through today. He just keeps getting better and better and better."

(Cheer.)

"It's a limited supply. If we sell the limited supply, we'll have to go back out to the truck and get another limited supply."

(Laugh.)

Why fifty songs? They were pretending it was George's fiftieth anniversary in the business. And while it had been fifty years since his first hit, it had been fifty-six since he told his first father-in-law he was a singer and not a house painter.

Three songs later, there was something else to sell. Meat.

"We're tryin' to catch up with Jimmy Dean," said Barry, as he pitched George Jones Country Sausage.

"I don't need the money," George chimed in, "but my creditors do."

(Laugh.)

Big Close.

Barry: "You'll never have a no-show for breakfast as long as you get George Jones Country Sausage."

George: "Only contains pure pork."

Barry: "Pure pork."

George: "No possum."

Barry: "No possum."

(Laugh.)

From the stage that night, George, with the help of Barry and Sheri, pitched CDs, sausage, and White Lightning, his own brand of bottled water. In the lobby, he was selling more CDs, key chains, videos, mouse pads, license plates, T-shirts, and hats. It may look small-time, but in a typical year, an insider told me, they make about a half-million dollars selling merchandise.

Around about now might be a good time for the purists to start pretending Hank or Bill Monroe or Jimmie Rodgers—somebody—is spinning in his grave. "All anybody cares about anymore is making a buck," they wail.

But George Jones is far from the first country singer to lend his name to a product and, when it comes to commercialism, the biz has seen a whole lot worse. George Jones

Country Sausage is nothing. There was a time when instead of naming the products after the singers, the singers were named after the products. Ernest Tubb was once dubbed the "Gold Chain Troubadour" by sponsor Gold Chain Flour; a Texas trio known as the Aladdin Laddies was the namesake of the Aladdin Mantle Lamp Company until an executive from a flour mill became the group's manager. The Laddies then became the Light Crust Doughboys. And these weren't some no-talent cowpokes who sold their souls to the devil. They were pioneers in western swing led by a guy named Bob, who soon would make history with his group Bob Wills and His Texas Playboys. In country music, when the money is right, names change and so does the music.

"All country musicians are commercial," wrote music critic Terry Teachout in the *New York Times*, "but some are a lot more commercial than others, and the two camps have been at war ever since Jimmie Rodgers cut his first 78's for Victor."

Listen to producer Billy Sherrill. "If you make a record, what goes on in the back of your mind is, 'I wonder how much I can make outta this thing?,'" said Sherrill. "And people that say different lie. That's the truth. It's what you do. It's where you make your livin'. So you do it to make money."

"Pluperfect awful." That's how then OKeh Records talent scout Ralph Peer described Fiddlin' John Carson's recordings in 1923. But Peer became a big fan after Carson emerged as one of country music's earliest recording stars.

Throughout its history, the kind of music coming out of Nashville has always been as much about sales as inspiration.

Duh.

Country music purists would like to forget about the business side, seeing it, as Bill Ivey once wrote, "as merely an occasional intrusion into what is essentially an artistic process."

Not so much.

"If you wanta be artistic, you can sit down in your den and enjoy it with a few of your friends," said Larry Butler, who was Kenny Rogers's producer in the "Lucille"/"Gambler" days. "If you wanta make royalties, you learn the business."

Like all popular art, country music has a split personality, with art on one side and commerce on the other. You can't have one without the other. Not that critics don't try.

"By now everyone who cares even casually about true country music knows the story of how Nashville was taken over by evil robots—it happened sometime in the sixties, seventies, eighties, or nineties, depending on who's telling the story—and how country radio subsequently went to hell in a multimillion dollar handbasket," wrote Stephanie Zacharek on Salon.com.

To state the obvious, without the existence of these "evil robots"—what the purists see as the satanic forces ruling both Nashville's Music Row and the labels in New York and L.A.—there would be no records, and the music, "true" or otherwise, never would have made its way out of hills and hollers and honky tonks onto a jukebox near you. Think Polk Brockman, the Atlanta furniture dealer who insisted Ralph Peer record Fiddlin' John Carson in the first place, did it to preserve what one scholar called "a vanishing culture?" Nah. Brockman figured he could sell more record players to rednecks if they could play their kind of music on the new-fangled machines.

"I don't ever look at a thing as to what I think about it. I always try to look at it through the eyes of the people I expect to buy it," Brockman told interviewers in 1961.

"This is a business. A business. A business. A business," said Tandy Rice, onetime manager of Tom T. Hall.

There are models for art-for-art's-sake, creative enterprises. First, consider the "business" of literary fiction. At the time the prestigious National Book Awards for fiction were handed out in 2004, four of the five finalists had sold "fewer than two thousand copies," according to David Segal in the *Washington Post*.

"The evening's theme, if it could be said to have a theme, was the alarming irrelevance of literature," wrote Segal.

The threat of irrelevance doesn't seem to bother some art-for-art's-sake classical music composers like Charles Wuorinen who see not catering to the audience as a badge of honor.

"You've denounced trends in composition to please the crowd, to write entertaining music to the detriment of music as art, pretty strongly," *New York Times* reporter Daniel J. Wakin said to Wuorinen in 2005.

"As I've said a million times, there has been an attempt, largely successful, to confuse what you might call art and what you might call entertainment," replied Wuorinen. "Entertainment is that which you receive without effort. Art is something where you must make some kind of effort, and you get more than you had before."

"It couldn't be clearer or more concise than that," chimed in James Levine, Musical Director of the Boston Symphony, "and that's absolutely right."

"There are things that are worth more and things that are worth less," Wuorinen told the *Times*. "But to say . . . the person who sticks a microphone in his mouth and sings a rock song is the equivalent of a highly trained opera singer, for example—it's just nonsense."

Take that, Bruce Springsteen.

So if not the audience, then who gets to decide what's "nonsense" and what's not, to sort out "the things that are worth more and things that are worth less"? The artist, wrote late Columbia University professor Lionel Trilling, "ceases to be the craftsman or the performer, dependent on the approval of the audience." Trilling says further, "His reference is to himself only, or to some transcendent power which—or who—has decreed his enterprise and alone is worthy to judge it."

So artists don't need a traditional audience. First they create something using those "transcendent" powers Lionel was talking about. Then they alone get to decide if it's any good. "As for the artist," continues Trilling, "even while he asserts his perfect autonomy and regards his audience with indifference, or with hostility and contempt, he is sustained by the certitude that he alone can provide what the audience deeply needs."

The message: forget sales. Do your own thing.

Now I doubt that things have ever really worked this way, even in Lionel Trilling's world, but it seems today's artists want to make damn sure their work is being judged by the smallest group of like-minded people possible. (And who could blame them?)

The artists would probably call these folk enlightened or smart or hip. I'd call them biased. Whatever. The point is, the general public is not included.

So from the lofty heights of the ivory tower, critics have left the people making the music with only two choices. First, there's the purist's route where they say to hell with the audience and risk "alarming irrelevance." Second, there's the charlatan, commercial route, where they say to hell with art and try to please the crowd.

In the real world where the music is being made, there's a middle ground. We'll call it "the Billy Sherrill exception." Here's how John Harbison, the Composer in Residence at the Pittsburg Symphony explained it in that conversation with Charles Wuorinen and others reported in the *Times*: "It's possible for people who intend to always entertain [like Billy Sherrill] to produce something that is very perceptible as art, and by contrast it's also possible for people who are intending to make very high art to produce nothing more than entertainment."

So commerce does not necessarily destroy art. Money and art can, and often do, mix. As for Billy Sherrill, a funny thing happened on the way to the bank—"Almost Persuaded," "Stand By Your Man," "He Stopped Loving Her Today," and on and on and on. This man who, to hear him tell it, was just trying to churn out enough hit records to pay the mortgage, ended up making art.

Who knew?

•   •   •

Finally, consider Jeff Koons, the visual artist perhaps most famous for the, shall we say, "overblown," forty-two-inch-tall figurine of Michael Jackson holding his pet chimp Bubbles. We're talking a major shiny object.

Commercially produced? Oh yeah, and worse. Much worse.

"Kitschy," wrote British art critic Matthew Collings, while still rating Koons "super-talented." *Time* art critic Robert Hughes was less kind. He agreed the piece was kitsch, calling it "syrupy, gross, and numbing," but didn't see that as a good thing. Koons, he wrote, was "transparently on the make" and that disqualified him as an artist. Koons, ranted Hughes, was "a starry-eyed opportunist par excellence."

Not a problem.

Speaking in *Art News*, pro-Koons art historian Robert Pincus-Witten said, "Jeff recognizes that works of art in a capitalist culture inevitably are reduced to a condition of commodity."

Translation: sooner or later all art is for sale.

And, Pincus-Witten continued, "What Jeff did say was, 'Let's short-circuit the process. Let's begin with the commodity.'"

Translation: If we are going to sell the sucker sooner or later, why not just put it up for sale at the get-go?

So even Koons admits he's a capitalist swine. The point? So what? Who cares about the sins of the artist? Tell us what the art is guilty of. Cue scholar Joli Jensen.

"Is something that is commercially produced necessarily bad? Is something uncommercially produced necessarily good?" she asks.

No and no.

If the art is good, it doesn't matter if Koons or Salvador Dali (to pick another likely suspect) is a "starry-eyed opportunist" "transparently on the make." Likewise, if the music is good, it doesn't matter who is and who isn't in it for the money. So the critics need to shut up about everybody's bank account and just listen to the damn music.

3

THE COUNTRY MUSIC DIALECTIC

The music industry has a pendulum that swings from
pop to traditional. There is nothing new under the sun.
—EVELYN SHRIVER, President, Bandit Records

I don't know about you, but right about now I'm feeling down-
right superior to Charles Wuorinen, Lionel Trilling, and that
whole elitist crowd who are so hopelessly sequestered in their
various ivory towers. Thank God I'm a country boy and all that.
Trouble is, first, I'm not really a country boy and, second, many
a country music purist shares a Wuorinen-like disdain for the
audience. They too want their music to be judged by the smallest
group of like-minded people possible, in this case traditionalists,
people who prefer fiddles to violins, Gretchen Wilson to Faith
Hill. Like classical composer Wuorinen, these purists are saying, "Forget the audience, we know better." And using a kind of
reverse snobbery, they argue that if a song is popular, it must be
crap. And if it's really, really popular, it's really, really crap.

"A sense of artistic gloom rises like a mist whenever country music stumbles on good times," wrote Bill Ivey a couple of
decades back. "And that sense is accompanied by nostalgic long-
ing for another era, in which country music held a truer course."

"Writing [a song] for wide accessibility and popularity, this is
perceived by intellectuals and country music fans alike as a bad
thing," wrote scholar Joli Jensen in *The Nashville Sound*.

Terry Teachout from the *New York Times* seems to think
there is a conspiracy afoot.

It's a never ending cycle: first, "hard" country singers like
[Jimmie] Rodgers, Hank Williams, and George Jones create

strong, emotionally true styles. Then shrewd musical entrepreneurs water these styles down for painless consumption by a larger and more affluent audience. In time, the gruel becomes so washy that a rebellious new generation of tradition-minded upstarts moves in and takes over.

This melodramatic soft-versus-hard, "washy gruel" versus "strong, emotionally true" way of telling the country music story has a long, long history. In 1910, critics worried "authentic 'traditional' music" was being crowded out by "crassly commercial, string-band styles." In 1929, real country music was pronounced "finished" altogether. In the forties, "purists" worried the "honky-tonkers" were forcing out "the now-established string bands." (All this reported by Vanderbilt's Richard Peterson in *Creating Country Music*.) And in the fifties and sixties, country music reportedly was threatened by rock 'n' roll and the Nashville Sound.

This battle over what is and what ain't real deal, authentic country music, continues in the twenty-first century. The two big winners at the 2005 CMA awards were Australian hunk Keith Urban, who was named Entertainer of the Year, and Lee Ann Womack, who took home three awards including Album of the Year and Single of the Year. Urban, or "Bon Jovi with fiddles," as one critic called him, won on the back of records that crossed over to the pop charts, and Womack for her traditional country album *There's More Where That Came From*.

"Country Goes Pop, Stays Traditional," read the schizoid headline in the Nashville *Tennessean* the next morning. It was a headline which would have fit, at one time or another, in every decade for the past forty years as pop-goes-the-country artists like Glen Campbell, John Denver, Olivia Newton-John, Anne Murray, Kenny Rogers, and, dare I say, the fabulous Faith Hill, walked away with major CMA awards.

Truth is, folks on Music Row have always been willing to do whatever works for the song and the singer. Or as Billy Sherrill put it: "You just gotta do what you gotta do, what you think helps the record."

So, pop. Traditional. Whatever.

Okay, here are the same facts, used to tell a different story, courtesy (mostly) of Richard Peterson. First off, the old notion that "the development of country music" can be traced by a straight line "from more folklike [traditional] to more commercial and poplike music" is simply untrue. The two styles have forever coexisted.

As far back as the 1850s, soft country fodder like Stephen Foster's "Swanee River," "Old Kentucky Home," and "Oh Susanna" was being played and sung alongside hard country, reported Peterson. The simple fact is soft country music has been around just as long as hard country music. And that's a good thing, argued Peterson, because, over the years, the "dialectic interplay" between soft and hard, pop and traditional, "has served to continually revitalize country music." (A quick refresher: in a *dialectic*, two direct opposites dubbed the *thesis* and *antithesis* collide, then combine to create a third thing called a *synthesis* that contains the best of both.)

So far, word hasn't gotten out about the country music dialectic, and every time soft country music rises to the top of the charts, the wailing and gnashing of teeth soon begins amid complaints that finally, really this time, no kidding, country music as we know it is on the eve of destruction.

"Well, they tried to get rid of it, I don't know how many times," George Jones told an interviewer in 2007. "This time I guess they just about succeeded."

Since this is country music where what you had for breakfast is considered legitimate fodder for a song, it's not surprising that Nashville songwriters are all over this one. Here are a few lines from "Murder on Music Row" by Larry Shell and Larry Cordle.

> The almighty dollar
> And the lust for worldwide fame
> Slowly killed tradition
> And for that, someone should hang.

Over the years, there have been so many songs lamenting the passing of traditional country music, they qualify as a kind of subcategory. There's a seldom noted irony here. The continuing success of these songs contradicts their premise. (For example, "Murder on Music Row" was recorded by mainstream country stars George Strait and Alan Jackson and was on the charts for twenty weeks.)

Summing up, everybody needs to just chill. To continue growing, every generation of country music needs its Hank Williams *and* Eddy Arnold, its George Jones *and* Kenny Rogers, its Lee Ann Womack *and* Keith Urban, its Gretchen Wilson *and* Taylor Swift, its hard and soft country. Instead of whining, we should celebrate the existence of each, because both are necessary for country to evolve.

One last thing. Cutting hit records is never, ever simply a matter of the sellouts ("shrewd musical entrepreneurs") watering down "strong, emotionally true styles" "for painless consumption by a large and more affluent audience." If that were true, half the people in this town would be gazillionaires. I mean, where do I sign up? Instead what you have are a bunch of wannabes trying to copy the records that are selling—and that's a lot harder than it looks.

"A lot of people tried to copy what Billy [Sherrill] did," recalled Quonset Hut engineer Lou Bradley in *Mix* magazine. "And they'd hire that studio, they'd hire the same engineer, and they'd hire the same musicians and background singers, but they wouldn't get it, because they were listening to the end result, and the end result was what you heard *after* you walked the path to get there."

"The hardest thing on earth to do is talk about what you do. That's the hardest thing," Billy Sherrill told me. "The hardest thing I ever do is something like talking to you about this. Doing it is fun and it was, but trying to explain to somebody why you did it is hard. Because you don't know why."

I don't want to embarrass Billy, but that's spoken like a true artist.

4

THE LESSON OF PADUCAH

There's the recording musician and the everyday picker.
They're really not the same. A guy that's really great on a show
may not be any good at all on a session and vice versa.
— PETE WADE, "He Stopped Loving Her Today" guitarist

Meanwhile back in Nashville, country music's greatest singer, George Jones, stepped to the microphone to sing country music's greatest song, "He Stopped Loving Her Today," in country music's most revered venue, the Ryman Auditorium. It should have been a national-holiday, unlimited-hall-passes, chocolate-chip-cookies-right-out-of-the-oven kind of moment. George Jones is the real deal in the flesh, the country singer most likely to be cited by the I-know-it-when-I-hear-it crowd. And so as George stood there on the edge of the Ryman Auditorium stage, seconds away from singing the opening notes of "He Stopped Loving Her Today," you can't fault me for expecting magic.

Dream on.

Didn't happen. Not for a second. Not for a note. Oh, George sang, all right, and the audience gave him a standing "O," but the sound pouring out of the speakers at the Ryman had little to do with the recording I'd been listening to for thirty-some years. This would all make sense A.P., "After Paducah," but at the time, I was the-man-in-the-red-velvet-suit-means-well, but-I-can-see-his-beard-is-taped-on, gotta-keep-my-mouth-shut-so-Mom-won't-find-out-there-is-no-Santa-Claus, S-A-D, *sad*. And there were no presents under the tree to soften the blow.

• • •

Ten months had passed since The Ryman Disappointment and George was set to appear in Paducah, Kentucky. Paducah was easy. Not only is the city within easy driving distance of Nashville, about two hours, it is also a no-sweat in-and-out thanks to a population of under thirty thousand.

I had never been to Paducah, but I grew up hearing about it because my father, who helped build "the bomb" in Oak Ridge, used to go up there all the time in the fifties to visit a plant that produced the highly enriched uranium used in reactors and nuclear weapons. The plant is still there, but today Paducah wants to be known for making quilts, not bombs.

Home of the American Quilter's Society and the National Quilt Museum, Paducah has taken to calling itself Quilt City U.S.A., and since 2000 the city has tried to lure artists to town with its "Artists Relocation Program," offering no-down-payment, low-interest home loans.

Having learned nothing at the Ryman, I wanted to go to Paducah and take another shot at finding the magic. Maybe George or the sound man or the Jones Boys or a certain listener writing a book were having an off night in Nashville.

The sun was down by the time we reached the Paducah environs.

"I guess it's exit sixteen, not fourteen," Judge-John-Brown told the driver, correcting himself. "You just get off and you turn right, follow the road in. And if you want me to, you can pull over and I'll drive after you get off 'cause I've been here several times and kinda know where we're going."

The operative word being "kinda."

"I've got directions," I said.

"Ah, we don't need 'em," said the Judge.

So there we were, wandering around Paducah in the dark in a steady rain looking for the Executive Inn or "the E," as locals call it, a sprawling, 434-room hotel on the banks of the Ohio River where George would be singing that night.

All talked out after two hours in the car, there was soon nothing but Kristofferson's "windshield wipers slapping time" as we worked our way around the sheer outer walls of the humongous

Executive Inn looking for an opening. In the dark, the driver made a wrong turn into an empty lot and then backtracked, gravel crunching beneath the tires. Finally we rounded a corner and stumbled upon the parking garage. If "the E" had a formal entrance, we never found it.

Inside, the hotel was passing strange. A soaring, Hyatt-like lobby had been subdivided at floor level into a rabbit warren of retail shops and rented offices. Although huge, the place had a mom-and-pop feel to it and not in a we-love-you, try-the-meat-loaf kind of way. It was more like the place was a little too much to handle. Disheveled. Disorganized.

We followed the white hair and baseball cap crowd down a windowless corridor filled with roiling cigarette smoke to a packed Las Vegas–style showroom that seated about nine hundred. Up front, blue upholstered banquets in concentric semi-circles rose from the stage before giving way to tables toward the back of the room.

Judge-John-Brown again scored backstage passes, but here backstage turned out to be ten or twelve folding chairs set up to the left of the stage. George stuck his head out the door of the real backstage area long enough to tell the Judge Nancy wasn't there: recovering from disk surgery back in Nashville, he said. Without Nancy the pre-show fan club meet-and-greet never got off the ground, and George would end up apologizing for the lapse.

We settled into our seats way in the back as George kicked off the show at 8:45 with "Why Baby Why?" He continued with "Once You've Had the Best," "The Race Is On," and "Bartender's Blues," the same opening rundown as the Ryman.

"No swinging on ropes on this stage," he said, taking a swipe at Garth.

During "Choices," photos from the Jones family album were projected on the video screen: shots of George's parents, the famous photo of him as a boy strumming a guitar on the streets of hometown Beaumont, Texas; a shot of him wearing a white cowboy hat in an early publicity photo; a two-shot with Nancy.

George attempted a shout out to Judge-John-Brown from the stage. "Hey Judge-Joe-Brown!" he said.

Our tickets had us sharing a table for eight in the next to last row. Back there in the cheap seats the folks had been sipping for some time and were paying more attention to each other than what was happening on stage. I wandered down to the "back-stage" folding chairs, but didn't like the sight lines or the sound and ended up standing about halfway back in the far left aisle waiting for the magic, but bracing myself for what I thought might be "The Paducah Disappointment." Then came "Blues Man," a song from George's *Hits I Missed . . . and One I Didn't* album.

On the CD it was a duet with Dolly. In Paducah, he sang it with Sheri of Barry and Sheri, sang the hell out of it, in fact. Sang it as only George Jones could sing it.

So I started drinkin'
And took things that messed up my thinkin.'
I was sure sinkin'
When you came along.

This performance was the real deal: the magic I was looking for, the reason I get up off my couch and go to a concert. George put his heart into it and took me right along with him. Not that this one song would be enough to convince me to make a habit of this concert-going thing. "Blues Man" was the exception. The Paducah rendition of "He Stopped Loving Her Today" ended up being just as lackluster as the Ryman version—and that got me to wondering.

I checked out George's song list. At least a third of the songs in the Paducah show were, if not finger-on-the-trigger, then at least bottle-to-the-lips sad. Toward the end, George sang a medley that began with the emotional one-two punch of "The Window Up Above" ("Our marriage was all wrong") and "The Grand Tour" ("She left me without mercy"), then rope-a-doped the audience into complacence with the upbeat "Walk Through This World With Me" ("Share all my dreams") before delivering the knockout punch with the standalone tune "She Thinks I Still Care" ("I saw her, then went all to pieces").

These songs are all, pretty much, a testimony to the utter and complete hopelessness of long-term relationships. If George made like Billie Holiday—who, as the story goes, "never sang a note she didn't mean"—there's no telling what kind of emotional toll it would take to sing that lineup of songs every night. Can any singer dredge up that kind of real emotion every time over a lifetime of performances and live to tell the tale? I don't think so. While performers may give a particular song the emotional full-speed-ahead (like George did in Paducah on "Blues Man"), I'm thinking no way they can do it every time or even most of the time.

So if you're wanting magic, the concert stage nearest you may not be the place to find it, whoever the singer, whatever the song. Emotionally no performer can or will, or should be expected to, really now, open a vein for us and bleed on cue on a nightly basis. I'm guessing the best strike a balance between feeling it and maintaining their mental health. Others fake it.

Not to worry.

There is a way to experience the real thing every night, and not only on "Blues Man" but on "He Stopped Loving Her Today" and every other Jones hit from the past fifty years. It's called a "recording."

Recordings are wondrous things. Singers, producers, musicians, and engineers go into the studios and do whatever they need to do to record heartfelt, authentic renditions of songs that can be played over and over and over.

"Patsy's been crying on every one of these records, really crying," Owen Bradley once told Patsy Cline's husband as he was asking him to leave the studio. "I don't want to break the mood. You stay out of there."

The magic of recording means if you want to hear George Jones suffer along with the dear departed in "He Stopped Loving Her Today," you're not at the mercy of a road-weary crew trying to reinvent the wheel at some funky hotel called "the E" in Paducah—by God—Kentucky.

And while it's always a thrill to see the stars in person, if you're like me, you can count on one hand the number of concerts where the live performance lived up to the record. Off the top of my head: Bette Midler in Knoxville in the seventies—yes, that's the seventies—when Barry Manilow was still her music director; Delbert McClinton, my idol, somewhere in Nashville— the Cannery?—in the early eighties; Vince Gill all alone on stage filling in for a hoarse Delbert McClinton at a benefit for the Nash- ville Children's Theater circa 2004; Tony Bennett at the Ryman Auditorium in 2006. Some total losses: Bob Dylan, Diana Ross, and Michael Jackson. I'll spare you the details.

There are exceptions, of course, but night after night, if the choice is live or Memorex, opt for the recording. Why? Because the recording is almost always better than the live performance.

Why is the record better? Short answer: better musicians under better conditions.

Long answer part one: records are cut by session musicians who most agree are the best musicians on the planet.

"We were held to a higher standard," said legendary session bass player Bob Moore.

"A stage musician and a studio musician is two different types," said session pianist Pig Robbins. "The stage guy—y'know— is probably more flashy and plays a whole lot more than you need to. On a record, you pick your spots instead of everybody filling in all at once. Just a different, a whole different attitude."

What's more, the so-called "session" or "studio" musicians are often playing irreplaceable instruments no one would even think about subjecting to the wear and tear of the road.

Long answer part two: modern recording studios are a con- trol freak's dream. Every note played, every syllable sung, every sound wave generated, is ultimately under the absolute and com- plete control of the producer. So Nashville's finest do it over and over and over until the recording sounds like everybody was hav- ing a great day. And if they weren't? No problem, thanks to tech- niques like "tuning."

"A majority of the artists [singers] are tuned. And when you hear 'em live, you can tell which ones they are," said songwriter/ producer Bobby Braddock. "I'm talkin' about goin' in with com- puters after the singer has made a performance and tuning his voice"—taking a wrong note and electronically "tuning" it into the right one.

There's another reason records sound better than live performances. Often the only person on stage who was even *there* when the recording was created is the star. Only after the producer, session musicians, and engineers get a song perfect, does the road band, the band you hear at concerts, learn the tune.

"George Jones, he had his own band. But they didn't do the records," said Bob Moore. "They put the record on the player and they would learn everything we had played. It was our ideas that they took and played."

Lick for lick.

"The audience out there, they wanta hear it the way they're used to hearing it, the way they heard it on the radio," said longtime *Hee Haw* musical director Charlie McCoy.

So after a song is recorded, the creativity is pretty much over. In visual arts lingo, the recording of a song is the original and any subsequent stage performance, a print.

"That's a good analogy," said McCoy.

And in comparison to the studio original, the road "print" can be a stale, not-so-good, paint-by-numbers reproduction. Not that there aren't ways around the problem.

"We do enough improvisation, thankfully, that it feels pretty fresh for my band and me," Brad Paisley told Beverly Keel of the *Tennessean*. Still, "it's a challenge to keep the show fresh for his band and fans who have seen numerous shows," wrote Keel, "and still satisfy the desires of fans who want to see . . . [the hits] just like they've heard them on radio."

One last reason the record sounds better than the live performance. No matter who ends up on stage or how well they're playing, there's little chance a venue's sound system can deliver the control-freak-quality audio heard on the record, whether a performer is playing at a renowned concert hall or on a flatbed truck in the parking lot at the local shopping mall. So we shouldn't be surprised that "He Stopped Loving Her Today" didn't rise to the level of magic at the Ryman Auditorium in Nashville or "the E" in Pudacah. Oh, there can be the rare song like "Blues Man," and that rare singer like George Jones, where "the energy and the immediacy" of a stage performance, as songwriter Bobby Braddock put it, can rise above any record ever made. Blow you away.

But on a given night, on a given song, don't get your hopes up. Not that fans can't get caught up in the moment.

A fan at one concert told Braddock that the singer, whose CD Bobby had produced, sounded better live than he did on the record.

"I thought, 'You dumb ass,'" recalled Braddock. "'If you were listening, if you were listening to what you're seeing now, it would sound like crap.'"

And that is The Lesson of Paducah.

PART TWO

AUTHENTICITY, A.K.A. THE REAL DEAL

5

HILLBILLIES AND COWBOYS

A Hill-Billie is a free and untrammeled white citizen of
Alabama, who lives in the hills, has no means to speak of,
dresses as he can, talks as he pleases, drinks whiskey when
he gets it, and fires off his revolver as the fancy takes him.
—*NEW YORK JOURNAL*, April 23, 1900

Whatever you choose to call today's most virulent strains of country music—"hard core," "stone country," "the real deal"—George Jones is still the man. Producer Keith Stegall calls him "the source." Like Jimmie Rodgers and Hank Williams before him, back in the sixties the hard-livin', drink-it-if-you-got-it Jones came to personify authenticity. And in country music, that's huge.

"Authenticity has come to define country music more, perhaps, than any other musical genre," wrote Hugh Barker and Yuval Taylor in *Faking It: The Quest for Authenticity in Popular Music*.

"Country music is *not* rock. It is *not* pop. It is *not* jazz," wrote scholar Joli Jensen. So what is it, then? "Authenticity offers country music an identity—this is what country music is." The billboard version:

AUTHENTICITY
WHAT COUNTRY IS

Because of that identity, authenticity has become the critical measuring stick of everything associated with country music. Music, image, performance, and the people themselves: all are subject to an authenticity test.

In establishing that authenticity, "music and performance are vital," wrote Vanderbilt Sociology Professor Richard Peterson in his book *Creating Country Music: Fabricating Authenticity.* "The boots, the hat, the outfit, a soft rural Southern accent, as well as the sound and subjects of the songs, all help. Finally, being able to show a family heritage in country music is perhaps the strongest asset."

But there's trouble in Music City. When folks who haven't done the reading hear something described as authentic, they often assume there is a bloodline, a history that can be traced back to a source "where all movement ends and begins," as Columbia professor Lionel Trilling put it in his classic book *Sincerity and Authenticity.* But bloodline tests don't apply to many of the key elements of country music.

Consider traditional images. Say you're watching a music video of a good ole boy all dressed up in a cowboy hat, boots, and jeans, sitting on the front porch, strumming his guitar and singing one of those heartfelt hillbilly songs. Little about this scene has any basis in reality. Most everything that's "hillbilly" originated in the 1920s and can be traced to the stage of the Grand Ole Opry in Nashville and most everything that's "cowboy" originated in the 1930s and can be traced to the Republic Studios in Hollywood. And when that search is done, what you find is not an actual hillbilly or cowboy, but somebody's fanciful notion of what a hillbilly and cowboy might be. What they might look like, sound like, act like. The setting they might be in. How they might perform. What instruments they might play. Professor Peterson kindly called all this "fabricating authenticity." I call it "making stuff up."

"Few working cowboys played guitar or fiddled and sang," wrote Peterson, "and while a large number of Southerners of the 1920s were musical, most of them were not unlettered, shiftless hillfolk. Rather the singing cowboy and the hillbilly character were deliberately constructed images."

Contrivances.

The most influential fake hillbillies were largely the doing of WSM's George D. Hay, the creator and host of the Grand Ole Opry. In the early days of the Opry, Hay, himself playing the character of the Solemn Old Judge, led the radio audience to believe the show was put on by "a bunch of farmers who just came to town of a Saturday night," wrote Peterson. Why? Money, of course. Hay, also the WSM station manager, thought these down-home characters would appeal to unsophisticated rural listeners who were potential customers for National Life and Accident Insurance Company, the owner of WSM. In keeping with the hillbilly pretense, Hay often renamed musical groups and made them dress in what he thought were appropriate costumes.

Dr. Bate and His Augmented Orchestra became the Possum Hunters and the Binkley Brothers Barn Dance Orchestra became the Dixie Clod Hoppers. Both Bate, a physician who "wintered in Florida," according to historian Charles Wolfe, and his string band were forced to shed their business suits and dress like Hay's idea of hillbilly, complete with goofy hats and pants rolled up above the ankles. The Dixie Clodhoppers, whose two leaders were watch repairmen by trade, ended up in overalls and straw hats. These country bumpkin images were stolen from stock vaudeville characters of the day, wrote Peterson.

Most early Opry performers not only weren't hillbillies or farmers, they weren't even rural residents. They were "steadily employed residents of Nashville," according to Peterson, who cited examples of a barber, cigar maker, and railroad dispatcher. No hillbillies in sight.

As for the authenticity of the music, "He [Hay] wouldn't know the difference between 'Turkey in the Straw' and 'Steamboat Bill,'" an unidentified source told Peterson. "He liked rapid tunes because he thought the man making the most racket was making the most music."

Anybody in search of authenticity will have no more luck finding real singing cowboys. Like the hillbillies, they were pretty much invented, this time by Republic Studios.

Gene Autry, the man who put the "sing" in singing cowboy, was a popular radio crooner on the WLS National Barn Dance in Chicago before he migrated to Hollywood in 1934. A company that would become part of Republic Studios first signed John Wayne for the singing cowboy gig, calling him Singin' Sandy, but that didn't work out. Wayne couldn't sing a lick, so somebody else had to do the actual singing, and Wayne didn't like the work to start with.

"I've had it," Wayne reportedly told his boss. "I'm a god-damn action star, you son of a bitch. I'm not a singer. Get yourself another cowboy singer."

[Note to Young Journalists: any quote that sounds too good to be true likely is.]

Autry would eventually replace Wayne and become a national sensation, but when he tried to hold out for more money, Repub-lic signed up one Roy Rogers, born Leonard Slye, then a singer with the western group Sons of the Pioneers. This was in 1937. Rogers's immediate success scared Autry back into the Republic fold, and, by the end of the decade, Gene Autry was as "famous as Clark Gable and Gary Cooper," wrote Peterson.

Not a cowboy music fan? Think all this should be buried in the "Who Cares?" file? Patience. While singing cowboys like Autry and Rogers had very little lasting influence on the country music sound, they had a huge influence on the country music image. Take ole Hank.

On stage, Hank Williams, an Alabama boy who sang more like Roy Acuff than Gene Autry and preferred "hunting and fish-ing" to "riding and roping," always appeared in western wear, according to Peterson, even though he "never performed songs about the American West." So why did Hank and most other hillbilly singers of the era decide they wanted to look like Gene and the boys? The hillbilly image had been taking a beating in the national press for years. Here's an often quoted example found in the December 29, 1926, issue of *Variety*: "The 'hill-billy' is a North Carolina or Tennessee or adjacent mountaineer type of illiterate white. . . . The mountaineer is of 'poor white trash' genera. The great majority, probably ninety-five percent, can neither read nor write English. Theirs is a community all to themselves. [They are] illiterate and ignorant, with the intel-ligence of morons."

In the mid-thirties the success of Gene Autry "proved that it wasn't so much the music as the hillbilly style . . . that turned off a greater audience," wrote historian R. J. Young in *The Illustrated History of Country Music*. "Thus the hillbilly music-makers fol-lowed Autry's lead by simply changing their dress code. Straw hats and patched overalls were quickly replaced in many quarters with white Stetsons and starched and spangled cowboy outfits."

So you've got folk who are neither cowboys nor hillbillies wearing cowboy outfits and singing hillbilly songs. Made no sense, was "absolutely artificial," as historian Patrick Carr wrote in *Country: The Music and the Musicians*. But, as Joli Jensen pointed out, "the country music 'look' is, of course, no more or less authentic than any other stage costume."

Real or not, the cowboy garb worked exactly as planned. The singing cowboy image "made country music at least palatable to a 'sophisticated' audience that had previously jeered at it," wrote Young. "'Hillbilly' was out; 'Country and Western' was in."

"It certainly beat being labeled as backwoods dolts from the hills," wrote Carr in *Country: The Music and the Musicians*. "[And] it established a link of image between country people and cowboys that survives to this day."

But that jeering by sophisticated audiences that country singers wanted to avoid? It wouldn't subside for long. Not with Nudie around.

• • •

In the forties, Nudie Cohn, a Jewish, flyweight-boxer-turned-tailor from Brooklyn was hired to make costumes for the band of singing cowboy Tex "Smoke! Smoke! Smoke! (That Cigarette)" Williams and Nudie's Rodeo Tailors of North Hollywood, California, was born.

Nudie learned the art of tailoring while crafting G-strings for strippers in New York. In Hollywood his first company logo featured a naked woman "leaning against a fence, twirling a lasso whose coils spelled out the company name." When the cowboy costumes began to sell, Nudie cleaned up the logo, dressing the woman in cowboy duds—hat, short-sleeved bolero jacket, miniskirt, and boots—and added a six shooter.

By the late fifties, Nudie's brightly colored, rhinestone-encrusted, appliquéd, Mariachi band–inspired, cowboy-writ-large outfits were hillbilly chic and, Nudie, as music critic Nick

Tosches noted, had "taught a generation of country singers that lavender and orange" were matching colors. The so-called Nudie suit would go on to become a country music status symbol. Even George Jones succumbed.

For the cover of his 1967 *Walk Through This World With Me* album, George posed in a black wool Nudie suit. Detailing included elaborate, multicolored embroidery on sleeves and pants legs, and, on the jacket, appliquéd references to his first chart-topping song, "White Lightning," in the form of gold and rhinestone lightning bolts, and moonshine jugs with X's. This sort of elbow-to-the-ribs, kitsch literalism was typical of Nudie suits. A Porter Wagoner version had appliquéd wagon wheels; Ferlin Husky, appliquéd husky dogs; and rock star Gram Parsons of the country-rock Flying Burrito Brothers, asked for and got appliquéd marijuana leaves and Benzedrine pills. That was a real knee-slapper until the twenty-six-year-old Parsons died of a drug overdose in 1973.

The Nudie suit would eventually backfire. The cowboy attire that performers first donned in search of mainstream respectability would, in Nudie excess, bring country the very ridicule it was trying to live down. The Nudie suit screamed "White trash with money!" and gave the satin-sheets crowd something else to make fun of.

Were the critics right? Were Nudie suits tasteless? Are you serious? "The tastelessness of Nudie's creations is exquisite," as Mark Simpson wrote on ShowStudio.com.

Were the suits contrived? Yes. Camp? Yes. Authentic? Yes, that too. How can something be both contrived and authentic? It's guilt by association.

Over the years, the Nudie suit, the totally contrived cowboy style, came to mean "authentic" in country music, not because it had anything to do with real ridin' and ropin' cowboys, but because it had everything to do with real pickin' and grinnin' singers. Performers like Ernest Tubb, Lefty Frizzell, Little Jimmie Dickens, the Maddox Brothers and Rose, and, yes, even Hank himself made the Nudie suit a symbol of authenticity. So the Nudie suit is authentic not because of some cowboy bloodline, but because of the company it keeps. Same goes for all cowboy attire.

Performers like Hank Williams who are perceived as "the real deal," often dictate what is authentic. So Hank is not seen as authentic because he's wearing a cowboy outfit, but rather the cowboy outfit is seen as authentic because Hank is wearing it. No matter where the idea of wearing cowboy duds came from, Hank himself became the enduring source of authenticity. So today when somebody like Brad Paisley slaps on that cowboy hat, it's a way of saying "I'm a country singer." The cowboy hat that was once contrived has been made authentic.

The same kind of thing has happened to stage sets. Honky tonks are in and hay bales, wagon wheels, and cornfields have pretty much disappeared. The barn motif lives on, at least on the Grand Ole Opry.

At the George Jones show at the Ryman, you could see ghosts of a Nudie suit in George's stage wear. But the subdued, sparkling embroidery on his western cut, black suit jacket was not in the same league as the flamboyant rhinestone-cowboy outfits of the past. How diluted was George's look? Not even the country club crowd would call it tacky. Proof came the next day in a two-page Perry Ellis ad in the way-glossy, *Sunday New York Times* spring fashion supplement, where this David Bowie–looking model was sporting a black, spangled jacket that was the fraternal twin of the one George wore the night before. If anything, the Perry Ellis version was more country, with its wider lapels and more elaborate paisley print.

While most modern performers have backed off on the flamboyant cowboy costumes, a cowboy-lite image still reigns supreme as subdued western wear continues to be the fashion. Mega stars Kenny Chesney, Brad Paisley, and Tim McGraw all sport cowboy hats, jeans, and boots. Meanwhile most of the women (other than Dolly and Loretta) seem to be going the mainstream designer route. At one Academy of Country Music awards the ladies paraded about in designer gowns by Cavalli, Monique Lhuiller, Marc Bauer, Maz Azria, and Sandy Spika. Even self-proclaimed "redneck woman" Gretchen Wilson succumbed to designer fever, ordering her dress online from Frederick's of Hollywood. That, as they say in the reporting business, is a "telling detail."

6

COUNTRY CRED

(So what makes you country?)
Well, I think either you are or you're not. And I think if you're
not and you try to be, you'll be recognized as an imposter.
—LARRY BUTLER, producer

(A man in a suit leads two men onto a plowed field.)
"See boys, this farmer still has his culture and that's scary; his
roots, based in independence; his rebelliousness; his *country-
ness*, if you will. So what do they do about that? Well, that's
where the multi-media corporations step in. They begin to
bombard their new company man with caricatures and ste-
reotypes of himself—*Gomer Pyle, Dukes of Hazard, Beverly
Hillbillies, Hee Haw*, and so on and so forth—'til finally he
can't trust his own reality. He don't know what it is no more.
He starts *acting* country instead of *being* country."
—FROM *THE ACCOUNTANT*, winner of the 2001 Oscar for Best Live
Action Short Film, written and directed by Ray McKinnon

If you want to be in the country music biz, it's not enough to write
it, perform it, record it, and sell it, you also have to live it. Everybody from the label chief to the session musician is expected to
have personal authenticity, a country version of the rap artist's
"street cred"—call it "country cred"—if they want to be accepted
by fans and peers.

"The verbal accent, vocabulary, grammar, and prior rough
work experience affirm that a person is from the great geographic
cradle of country music and hasn't let education get the better of
working-class identification," wrote Vanderbilt professor Rich-

ard Peterson. "Performers [and others] without this full pedigree have to do special authenticity work to gain acceptance."

Either that or lie about it.

• • •

Case Study Number One. In 2002, an interview with the late, great Harlan Howard appeared in *Guitar Pull: Conversations with Country Music's Legendary Songwriters* by Philip Self.

Philip Self: "You were born in Harlan County, Kentucky. Is that where the name 'Harlan' comes from?"

Harlan Howard: "That's not true. I was born in Detroit, Michigan."

Seems Detroit wasn't country enough for Howard's handler when he was first getting started in the country music business in the early sixties.

"She says, 'You got a good name, but we can't have you born up in Detroit, not and be a country songwriter.'"

Turned out Howard might have had some kinfolk in Kentucky going back "twenty, thirty, forty years."

"So we picked Lexington. That's all BS."

And some forty years later, Howard was still trying to get it all straightened out. Meanwhile, he had written his way into country cred by penning classics like "I Fall to Pieces" (with Hank Cochran), "I Got a Tiger by the Tail" (with Buck Owens), and "Heartaches by the Number."

Case Study Number Two. Several years back, John Grady, then president of Sony Nashville (a very, very big job in this town) taught a one-night-only adult education class he called "Dreams, Myths, Facts: The Record Business Today" at his kid's school.

"Call me 'Grady,'" he said.

Cool. Now ole "Grady" had been in the music business about thirty years at that point and he propped up album covers in the blackboard chalk tray showing some of the artists he had been involved with during his career: folks like MC Hammer, Kenny G, Whitney Houston, Bonnie Raitt, Shania Twain, the Dixie Chicks, and Gretchen Wilson. That's some credentials. But in Nashville it wasn't enough.

To impress the dozen or so no-name students in his class, Grady allowed as how he grew up in O'Neill, Nebraska, population 3,282, where some of his best friends were ranchers. The message: while he may have strayed with the likes of Kenny G and Whitney Houston, ole Grady still had country cred.

"I feel I have earned my pedigree," he said.

Yahoo.

Anyway, summing up: country cred, don't leave home without it. And if there's a little hypocrisy involved, hey, no big deal. Which brings us to Case Study Number Three.

Wanta be an authentic, real deal country singer? Listen to Hank.

"You got to know a lot about hard work," country's greatest icon, Hank Williams, told *Nation's Business* magazine. "You have got to have smelt a lot of mule manure before you can sing like a hillbilly."

First off, Hank Williams had a bad back and if he ever did much "hard work," there's no record of it. He formed his band, the Drifting Cowboys, and started singing on the radio in his early teens, and, according to *The Illustrated History of Country Music* "except for an interlude as a shipyard laborer, Williams never worked at anything but country music."

As for logging mule time, if that really had been a criterion for a country singer, again ole Hank wouldn't have qualified. Because of his bad back, "he couldn't have plowed even if there had been plowing to do," wrote Canadian journalist Robert Fulford.

While "Williams was pure country in dress, speech, humor, even food (he doused everything with ketchup)," reported biographer Roger Williams, he didn't grow up on a farm and he didn't spend a lot of time looking, as he once put it, "at the backside of a mule." In fact, Hank Williams was more at home in a bar than a barnyard and the only backsides he spent a lot of time looking at were swathed in silk.

So why lie? Country cred matters and, in the fifties, it was the farm and not the honky tonk that was the holy grail of country authenticity. Hank would change all that.

In his role as the leading light of the live-hard, die-young, and leave-a-beautiful-corpse crowd, Hank Williams would become the source of a whole new variety of authenticity that didn't have a damn thing to do with farms and mules. Jimmie Rodgers, the so-called Father of Country Music, gave him a leg up.

In *Faking It: The Quest for Authenticity in Popular Music*, authors Hugh Barker and Yuval Taylor credit Rodgers with pioneering the whole sing-your-life, autobiographical thing (that would become a given in country music) starting with his song "TB Blues" in the thirties.

"Got that old TB, can't eat a bite," Rodgers sang of the disease that would eventually kill him.

Hank Williams and his honky tonk cronies would take that autobiographical approach to a whole new level. When they weren't singing about drinkin' and foolin' around, they were drinkin' and foolin' around. And it was Hank, wrote Professor Peterson, who would make singing your life the norm as the honky tonk singer-songwriter came to replace the field-plowing yokel as the model of authenticity. And it was this honky tonk legacy that became the source of George Jones's authenticity. Like Hank, George paid his dues in a bar, not a barnyard.

Thanks to Hank and honky tonk pals like Ernest Tubb and Lefty Frizzell, for the first time in history, the music that had claimed to personify authenticity, that prided itself on being real, was no longer faking it. Unlike the contrived, totally fabricated hillbilly and cowboy images of the past, the honky tonk image was all too real and country music would soon have the broken hearts and broken dreams to prove it. Country cred was suddenly credible and Hank Williams was the prototype.

It would be tempting just to make Hank the starting point for country cred, Lionel Trilling's place "where all movement ends and begins," and be done with it. Going back farther in an attempt to establish authenticity you can get bogged down not only in the cowboy/hillbilly folderol, but in all sorts of tricky legitimate questions like: was Jimmie Rodgers's real claim to fame being the first performer "to make the ever-popular blues acceptable to white audiences," as folklorist Charles Wolfe has suggested? And what are we to think of Vernon Dalhart, born Marion Try Slaughter, the New York–based, slumming light opera singer who scored country music's first million-selling country record in 1924? Was he authentic? Did he have any country cred? And how'd Tex Williams get away with using those very "un-country," muted trumpets on "Smoke! Smoke! Smoke! (That Cigarette)," his number one country single in 1947?

Let's see: Jimmie Rodgers sang blues, jazz, pop, country: whatever it took to pay the bills. Biographer Nolan Porterfield claimed Rodgers is the "most enduring" popular singer of the twenties and thirties, so country music should be glad to have him whatever his claim to fame. Dalhart had even less country cred than Rodgers. Although a Texan by birth, Dalhart sang in any style and dialect that would sell before hitting it big as a pretend hillbilly singer. As for Tex Williams, he was one of those country hybrid, anything-goes, Western Swing guys. (The flip side of "Smoke! Smoke!" was "Roundup Polka.") Does that impact his country cred?

Just thinking about authenticity and country cred can make you nuts, and serious researchers who have been bold enough to take on the subject have ended up shaking their heads. That's what happens when you discover the likes of the genuine, one hundred percent authentic Emmett Miller. But authentic what? He was "a white man in blackface," as Nick Tosches wrote, "a hillbilly singer and a jazz singer both, a son of the deep South and a roué of Broadway." His music was "definable neither as country nor as blues, as jazz nor as pop, as black nor as white, but as both culmination and transcendence of those bloodlines and more."

Try and sort that out.

"Authenticity matters deeply to people, but when we examine the concept, it begins to disintegrate," wrote Joli Jensen in *The Nashville Sound.*

I'll say.

Still by stealing one of Professor Peterson's ideas we may be able to make a little headway. Remember his description of country fans as a kind of ethnic group that comes with a "way of life" and an "imagined place in society"? People trying to establish their country cred, their authenticity, are trying to prove they are part of that ethnic group. They're saying because of this, that, and the other thing, I'm one of you.

The dividing line between the cotton and satin sheet crowds used to be strictly class. No more. As country deejay Hugh Cherry told Professor Peterson: "anybody who is a hillbilly today is a hillbilly by choice." Yeah, but if it's a choice, are they really authentic? To be authentic, shouldn't "hillbilly" be what you *are*, not what you choose to be? If there is a choice involved, do we become like the man in *The Accountant*, that movie quoted at the beginning of the chapter, who "starts *acting* country instead of *being* country"?

Yeah, said Lionel Trilling in *Sincerity and Authenticity*, the classic, if ponderous, book on authenticity. (I read it so you won't have to.) "What destroys our authenticity is society," he wrote. As we adapt in response to "the opinion of other people," we start acting instead of being.

Trilling quotes English poet William Wordsworth: "Points have we all of us within our souls / Where all stand single." That's the individual's source of authenticity. Then things go terribly wrong, wrote Trilling. "The prescriptions of society pervert human existence and destroy its authenticity." He quotes English poet Edward Young: "Born originals, how comes it to pass that we die copies?"

It's easy enough to advise "To thine ownself be true," but as Trilling points out at length, the problem is figuring out who your "ownself" is. You can't be who you really are, as opposed to who you chose to be, until you figure out who you really are. Summing up: to be authentic, you have to find out who you really are and then be that.

Like I said, just thinking about authenticity can make you nuts.

One last source of country cred: personal suffering. Like British reporter Richard Dorment observed in *The Daily Telegraph*, for the true artist "failure and personal suffering [are] a badge of authenticity and a source of inspiration."

There's nothing uniquely country about that. The tortured-artist stereotype goes back a century or so. In fact, Dorment was not writing about country music performers at all, but the nineteenth-century painters featured in the *Rebels and Martyrs* exhibition (2006) at the National Gallery in London. Among the artists was Vincent Van Gogh, who chimed in on suffering in an 1888 letter to his brother Theo.

"The more I am spent, ill, a broken pitcher, so much more am I an artist, a creative artist," Vincent wrote, six months to the day before he hacked off part of his right ear.

So personal suffering is another tried and true route to authenticity. Like American poet Theodore Roethke said, "In a dark time, the eye begins to see."

•   •   •

Here's one last aside on country cred that all of us would like to forget. Beginning in the 1860s, minstrel shows were "one of the more popular urban musical sources" in the United States, according to country music historian Bill C. Malone. In the twenties, blackface singers Al Jolson and Eddie Cantor scored huge pop hits; in the twenties and thirties, *Billboard* even had a regular "Minstrelsy" column. Country music was not immune.

Early in their careers Jimmie Rodgers, Roy Acuff, Bob Wills, even singing cowboy Gene Autry performed in blackface. In 1933, according to Richard Peterson, the Grand Ole Opry's Lasses and Honey (later Jamup and Honey), "the widely known blackface vaudeville comedy act," were the headliners for the most expensive and, presumably, the most popular Opry show being booked out of the WSM Artists Service Bureau. By the forties it took "ten trucks, nine of them tractor trailers," to shuttle the Jamup and Honey tent show from town to town, according to Alanna Nash in *Country: The Music and the Musicians*. Blackface humor "remained a staple of country music stage shows on up to the fifties," reported Malone.

And the music featured in these shows was more than just novelty tunes. According to Nick Tosches, the music of twenties-era blackface performer Emmett Miller was the "birth-cry" of "all that has come to be called American music," including country. And Miller may have influenced Hank himself. Writing in *Book Forum*, critic Luc Sante reported that Hank's 1949 recording of

"Lovesick Blues" copied Miller's 1925 version "note for note and inflection for inflection." Maybe. Nick Tosches has claimed that Williams and Miller were once removed; that Williams copied a record by honky tonk singer Rex Griffin, who had copied Miller. Whatever. You can hear Miller's haunting version on line at red hotjazz.com/georgiacrackers.html.

So in country music, this blackface business isn't just the embarrassing footnote, the insignificant sidebar that we all might wish it to be. Quite the opposite. Truth is—don't try this at home—you could make the argument that white men in black-face have as much claim to country cred as hillbillies in overalls.

• • •

Case Study Number Four: a true story.

Hambone

It was the mid-fifties in small-town Tennessee and the frightened boy on stage looked to be about my age, ten or eleven.

("The body music called 'hambone' is made by using the hands to slap the thighs and the chest muscles," the *New York Times* reported in 1987.)

The boy was the closing act and he sat all alone, stage right, on a metal folding chair in the auditorium of what our principal, Mrs. Hobgood, liked to call the "Kingston Junior School."

("I keep trying for that playing-card-in-the-bicycle-spoke sound," hambone artist Derique McGee told the *Times.*)

The boy would follow songs, skits, and Dixieland music in a minstrel show put on by a local civic club. The Lion's Club, I'm thinking.

("The rhythmic patting motion of hambone has its origins in West African dance," reported the *Times.*)

White men in blackface. All for "a good cause."

("[Hambone] is a living bit of history, a neglected part of our heritage that flourished in minstrel shows and vaude-ville," Mr. McGee told the *Times*.)

The black boy sat all alone on a metal folding chair, stage right, waiting to perform.

("Sometimes I'm asked if I invented it," said Mr. McGee.)

●   ●   ●

Case Study Number Five.

This is a test. In the next ninety seconds you'll find out if you have country cred. The test comes by way of Emily Mitchell, who became Billy Sherrill's gal Friday the day after he discovered Tammy Wynette in 1966. Over the next couple of decades this secretary-turned-executive would see a few things.

"We had our bad boys—that's for sure," said Emily of the good old days.

So Emily showed up for work one day and she was met at the door by George Jones. George had spent the night at the office and, still drunk or high or something, he wanted her to listen to the new tunes he'd written. Well, drunk or not, the man was a big star.

"And so I just closed the door and called downstairs. I told them, 'If it's not important, please take a message,'" recalled Mitchell.

Turned out these weren't just any tunes.

"George was on cocaine really bad and he and I think it was Paycheck had been up all night long writin' gospel songs," recalled Mitchell.

Test over.

If you're thinking, "And your point?", congratulations, you have country cred. While outsiders may believe it's morally twisted to get wasted and write a rip-snorting gospel tune or two, you understand that such behavior is perfectly normal in the "Thank-you,-Jesus," "won't-you-please-come-forward?", Sunday-morning South. Can somebody give me an "Amen?"

7

JIMMIE AND THEM

Deliverance (Deluxe Edition) DVD (1972)
Now Accepting Advance Orders!
Four Atlanta businessmen's weekend canoe trip turns
into a desperate fight for survival in John Boorman's
riveting adaptation of James Dickey's novel.
—moviesunlimited.com

In the novel *Deliverance*, the town of Oree, Georgia, was a "sleepy and hookwormy and ugly, and most of all, inconsequential" mountain community with a Texaco station and "a little white-washed" town hall/jail combo.

In the movie *Deliverance*, the town of Oree, Georgia, was a jumping-off place for hillbilly hell. And before "the weekend they didn't play golf" was over, one of the four Atlanta businessmen (Ronny Cox) would die, another (Ned Beatty) would be sodomized, and the other two (Burt Reynolds and Jon Voight) would become killers as the four took on not only white water, but what one writer called "hillbilly evil incarnate."

The mountain setting for *Deliverance* was a variation on the clichéd myth that somewhere out there in the wilds of Appalachia there is, as Vanderbilt professor Richard Peterson described it, "an isolated, pristine remnant of a bygone natural environment, peopled by British American stock": the kind of place where all the authentic country music supposedly comes from.

"Sort of a giant cultural deep freeze," wrote folklorist Charles Wolfe, "where songs and music that had died out elsewhere were still preserved in their original state."

This fairy tale Appalachian region "in but not of America," peopled by "pure Anglo-Saxons," arose just after the Civil War in magazines back East, according to Ryan Bernard in his master's thesis "The Rise and Fall of the Hillbilly Music Genre," and, for whatever reason, it stuck.

But, of course, there is no "cultural deep freeze," never has been. Still the fantasy remains, and when people aren't making fun of that "pristine remnant of a bygone natural environment" (which is often), it can be depicted as either a kind of Eden—an idyllic culture untouched by modern life—or as a culture that is just plain "touched," as in aberrant, "crazy-as-a-hoot-owl," inbred. And for a brief moment, *Deliverance*, the movie, would have it both ways.

In the opening scenes of the film, the audience is introduced to a "demented country kid" named Lonnie. One eye "stared off at a furious and complicated angle," wrote Dickey, "while the sane, rational eye was fixed on something that wasn't there."

Shudder.

So Lonnie was the stand-in for the demonic Appalachia. But Lonnie would also be the stand-in for the idyllic Appalachia.

"Lonnie don't know nothing but banjo pickin'," said the "old man."

In the film, Drew (Ronny Cox) picked out a few notes, then a simple melody on his guitar. Lonnie answered and "after a while it sounded as though Drew were adding another kind of sound to every note he played, a higher, tinny echo of the melody," the narrator in Dickey's novel said. "And then it broke in on me that this was the banjo, played so softly and rightly that it sounded like Drew's own fingering." The banjo was being played by Lonnie, of course, the idiot savant.

"I'm lost," Drew shouted, as Lonnie left him behind and the "old man" clogged in the dirt beside the ancient, corroded gas pumps.

The contrast between the purity of the banjo playing and its nightmarish source results in one of the most memorable musical numbers in film history. Move over "Singing in the Rain," this is the "Dueling Banjos" scene from *Deliverance*.

But you knew that.

"Dueling Banjos" has since become a hillbilly anthem and today just playing the first five notes is enough to announce "there's a hillbilly in the house," for good or ill. Like the cowboy hat and the Nudie suit, the song, written in 1955, has earned its authenticity and now has as much country cred as the standard it replaced, in the popular mind at least, and that's saying something.

In his novel, James Dickey had Lonnie and Drew playing "Wildwood Flower," the old Carter Family chestnut. Most of us think of "Wildwood Flower" as the epitome of country music authenticity, but it's "an old pop song," according to scholar Charles Wolfe. It was written in 1860 by Joseph Philbrick Webster, a native of New Hampshire who also wrote the hymn "In the Sweet By and By."

Now may be the time to share what scholars have known for a long, long time. Most of the Carter Family repertoire, like "Wildwood Flower," fails any strict authenticity test. Think that's blasphemy? Same thing goes for the music of the Father of Country Music, Jimmie Rodgers, who has long shared billing with the Carters as an originator of country. But the bloodlines for the songs of both Rodgers and the Carters generally cannot be traced back to the British Isles or even to the mountains and ranches of the United States. Truth is, these two sources from which all commercial country music is said to have sprung were never what purists would call "stone country," not even on day one in Bristol.

• • •

Bristol, Tennessee, July 22, 1927. Ralph Peer, a talent scout for the Victor Recording Machine Company, came to town for a two week "recording expedition." While Peer would always try to make it sound like he'd ventured into the wilds of Borneo, the so-called Tri-cities, which include Bristol, Johnson City, and Kingsport, had a population of around thirty thousand people at the time, "making it the largest urban area in the Appalachians," wrote scholar Charles Wolfe, bigger even than Asheville. Peer set up his makeshift studio downtown at 408 State Street, and things were going slow, so the legend goes, until a story ran on the front page of the *Bristol News Bulletin*.

"Mountain singers and entertainers will be the talent used for record making in Bristol," read the front page newspaper item. The paper went on to mention that a local string band, the Stoneman Family, had earned thirty-six hundred dollars (then a small fortune) from record sales the year before.

"This worked like dynamite, and the very next day I was deluged with long-distance calls from the surrounding mountain region," Peer recalled in the early fifties. "Groups of singers who had not visited Bristol during their entire lifetime arrived by bus, horse and buggy, trains, or on foot."

Sure they did.

"Part of the Bristol legend implies that Peer just wandered into town, improvising and relying on serendipity for his discoveries," wrote Charles Wolfe in *The Journal of Country Music*.

Not so.

"The event was by no means a passive capturing of pure Appalachian folk music at a remote mountain hamlet full of barefoot hillbillies [as Peer would lead people to believe], but a calculated documentation of an emerging commercial art form in a bustling summer city," wrote Wolfe.

The Victor Recording Machine Company had not invested sixty thousand dollars to send Peer, two recording engineers, and a "half car load" of state-of-the-art recording equipment to Bristol on a wild goose chase. Most everything had been planned in advance.

"Peer probably had over sixty percent of his time already blocked out when he arrived in Bristol," reported Wolfe. "He knew many of the acts he was going to record, and in a few instances, he knew what he was going to record."

Peer had asked locals he knew to round up talent for the sessions. One talent scout was the leader of the Stoneman Family band, Ernest V. "Pop" Stoneman (like Peer a member of the Country Music Hall of Fame), and another Cecil McLister, a Bristol Victor record player dealer. McLister, who remembered Peer making two or three preliminary trips to Bristol before the actual recording session, claimed he was the one who hooked Peer up with the Carters.

"Peer [then] corresponded with A.P. Carter, setting up a recording date," reported Wolfe.

And just how country was the Carter Family: patriarch A.P., his wife Sara, and sister-in-law Maybelle? About half as country as Peer claimed.

"They wander in, he's dressed in overalls and the women are country women from way back there—calico clothes on," said Peer years later. "They looked like hillbillies."

Pure fiction. Why the B.S.? Then and now, authenticity sells.

"Peer and other early record company publicists in the twenties sought to authenticate their product by emphasizing its rural origins," wrote Wolfe.

Always the businessman, Peer was trying to convince the buying public that he was hawking simple mountain music made by simple mountain folk; music that would fit the marketing niche he himself had dubbed "hillbilly" several years before.

While most of the stories surrounding the "discovery" of the Carter Family are pure bull, Peer actually did stumble over Jimmie Rodgers—or vice versa—in Bristol.

"The best things in life seem to occur by pure accident," Peer wrote years later.

It seems Rodgers, who lived in North Carolina, just happened to be in Bristol buying a used car, a 1925 Dodge to be exact, at the same time as the Peer expedition, and he just happened to be staying in a boarding house on State Street near where Peer had set up his studio. Rodgers noticed a lot of musicians milling around, asked a few questions, and next thing you know he was auditioning for Peer. All this according to John Lilly, a Jimmie Rodgers historian. In Charles Wolfe's version, the *Bristol News Bulletin* story drew in the singer. Rodgers biographer Nolan Porterfield tells still another story. He has Rodgers finding out about the recording session while in Asheville and then seeking out Peer. Whatever. Jimmie got the word. Peer recorded the music.

In all, the Bristol Sessions would result in the recording of seventy-six songs by nineteen groups including the first recordings ever made by the Carter Family (August 1) and Jimmie Rodgers (August 4).

A few weeks later, after listening to the recordings, Peer recalled in 1953, "it was obvious that Jimmie Rodgers was the best artist uncovered by the Bristol expedition"—or any other exhibition for that matter. Rodgers would soon become Victor's biggest recording star.

"The commercialization of mountain folk music had come, and it had come with bewildering suddenness," wrote Charles Wolfe.

Wolfe noted that "Ralph Peer learned at that point that there was not only a market, but a ravenous market for this kind of music."

The Bristol Sessions have "come to signal the Big Bang of country music evolution," wrote Rodgers biographer Nolan Porterfield, "the genesis of every shape and species of Pickin' and Singin' down through the years."

The Carters cut six sides, but Rodgers only two—because he didn't have much of a hillbilly repertoire to work with. As Peer later told *Billboard*, "In order to earn a living in Asheville, [actually nearby Marion, North Carolina, at the time] he [Rodgers] was singing mostly songs originated by New York publishers—the current hits."

Pop songs.

Success wouldn't help Rodgers with the authenticity thing. In his later recordings, according to Charles Wolfe in *The Illustrated History of Country Music*, Rodgers would use "jazz bands, Hawaiian music ["Everybody Does It in Hawaii"], trumpets, clarinets, jug bands, and even, on one occasion, a musical saw."

Was Rodgers a sellout? By today's standards, sure. Join the club.

The Carters' music has been "widely praised for being 'honest,' 'true,' 'back to basics,'" reported critic William Hogeland in *Slate* in 2002. "[But while] the Carter Family may sound eternal and primitive now . . . much of their repertoire came from nineteenth century pop; much of the rest came from blues and ragtime, relatively new and often quite urbane forms in the twenties."

The Carters weren't a museum band, dedicated to keeping authentic country music alive. They were entertainers.

"Nobody was supposed to bow down and worship the Carters' 'Wildwood Flower' as something deeply and permanently authentic," continued Hogeland, "You were supposed to just lean back, close your eyes, and say 'nice.'"

So even at the "big bang," the moment that was the commercial beginning of all things country, the music wasn't anybody's idea of authentic. The Carters and Jimmie Rodgers? They'd play any damn thing.

While there may have been performers out there who played music that met everybody's definition of authentic, that music has never been a big part of the mainstream, commercial country music industry. The songs are museum pieces, sacred relics, curiosities. So forget 'em. Bye bye.

That leaves us with a problem. For country fans, nobody is thought of as more pure, authentic, and genuine than the Carter Family and Jimmie Rodgers; and if their music doesn't measure up, then maybe we need to find a new way to define authenticity. Here's a beginning.

For starters, no matter how much trouble we have nailing it down—Professor Peterson spent four pages just trying to come up with a definition—there is such a thing as authenticity. And thank goodness. Without it critics, journalists, and fans wouldn't have anything to fight about.

Next, forget bloodlines, whatever authenticity the music of the Carters and Rodgers did or did not have at the time when it was recorded should now be forgotten. Today that music should be thought of as authentic because the Carters and Jimmie Rodgers chose to play and sing it. Think of them as country music curators. So like the cowboy hat and Nudie suit and all the other country trappings that became authentic because of their association with Hank Williams and the rest, songs like the Carters' "Wildwood Flower" should qualify as stone country authentic, the real deal, simply because of their association with the Carters. So how do performers become curators?

Hank Williams's "route to success lay not in imaging—cornpone, sophisticate, western, whatever—but in the emotional power of the music itself," Patrick Carr wrote in *Country: the Music and the Musicians*.

For the most part, George Jones still puts on a traditional, "stand and strum" country show. And what else would you expect? Authentic country singers aren't supposed to "perform"—that's not real. They're supposed to respond to the feelings of the moment. Years back, one critic—can't remember who—bitterly denounced Garth Brooks for using the same gestures at the same place in the same song two shows running. He was accusing Garth of play acting. For some, that's a no-no and not just in country. In the online magazine *No Depression*, Grant Alden felt the need to defend rock star Bruce Springsteen from charges of inauthenticity after critics jumped his butt because "he puts on a show."

Critics want honest emotion.

Of course, the real measure of the music is not if the singer is really feeling it, but if the *audience* is really feeling it. The listener has gotta be buyin' what the singer is sellin'.

In his 1949 Opry debut, Hank Williams "was brought back for an unprecedented six encores by the screaming audience."

"He just absolutely laid the people out flat," steel guitarist Joe Talbot said. "The man just had something that all great stars have, the ability to connect with the emotions of the audience."

So what is it about country music in general and Hank Williams's music in particular?

"It can be explained in just one word: sincerity," Williams told *Nation's Business* magazine. "When a hillbilly sings a crazy song, he feels crazy. When he sings, 'I laid my mother away,' he sees her a-laying right there in the coffin. He sings more sincere than most entertainers because the hillbilly was raised rougher than most entertainers." (Why trust Hank's opinion? This time everybody seems to agree with him.)

In *Sincerity and Authenticity*, Lionel Trilling defines sincerity as "a congruence between avowal and actual feeling." Translation: when you're sincere, you feel the way you say you feel. Authenticity takes sincerity to another level, wrote Trilling, suggesting "a more strenuous moral experience than sincerity." With authenticity there is no "within and without," no how we feel and how we behave. They become one. While we may *act* sincere, said Trilling, we *are* authentic.

Summing up, then: to be authentic, country music, all music, has to come from the heart of the performer and rouse the heart of the listener. That makes the human heart the ultimate source of authenticity. Songs that effect that emotional transfer are authentic. People whether songwriters, singers, musicians, or producers that effect that emotional transfer are authentic. And finally, anything from a ten-gallon hat to a chartreuse Nudie suit can become authentic if associated with that handful of people who are masters of the art of moving an audience, curators like Jimmie Rodgers, Hank Williams, and George Jones.

PART THREE

THE NASHVILLE SOUND

8

VIOLINS FROM HELL OR THE SHORT, OFFICIAL, PRETTY-MUCH TOTALLY BOGUS HISTORY OF THE NASHVILLE SOUND

More than fifty years after the birth of the Nashville Sound, a lot of country music fans still get riled up at the sound of a roomful of violins. To them, a string section is inauthenticity personified. For all those who insist on holding this grudge, it's time to reveal who is really to blame for all the sweet-tea, string-laden confections that have been making their way out of Nashville and onto a radio playlist near you since the early sixties. And it's not who you think. Forget Owen Bradley and Chet Atkins and Billy Sherrill. They were all at best accomplices and anyway it wasn't the violinizers who caused all the upheaval. The real culprit was this no-good, low-down son of a brewer from Omaha. But that story will have to wait until the next chapter. We'll begin with the lie, the myth—the fairy tale spun from whole cloth.

• • •

In the early fifties country music was basking in its twangy, nasal, postwar, honky-tonk glory, when along came the evil rock 'n' roll and threatened its very existence. Run for your lives!

Some called it an "onslaught," others a "threat," still others a "crisis," but whatever they called it, everybody agreed: "Country music had to do something desperate and radical to survive," as a couple of folks put it in *The Illustrated History of Country Music.* That something was, of course, the Nashville Sound.

"I think we had to change," Chet Atkins told historian Robert Oermann.

"We were all just trying to survive," Owen Bradley said.

So how bad was this rock 'n' roll crisis? Here's one take from Wesley Rose of publisher Acuff-Rose as reported in *Country: The Music and the Musicians*: "At one disastrous point, the company spent only half days at the office with the entire staff adjourning to softball games every afternoon during the summer of 1957."

That's puzzling. If my company were at a "disastrous point," I might have considered laying people off instead of paying them to play softball. But, hey, I've never been much of a businessman.

"How bad was it?" item two, again from *Country: The Music and the Musicians*: The same year Wesley and company were playing softball, RCA announced the creation of a new Nashville office to be headed by Chet Atkins.

"How bad was it?" item three, from BMI's online history of Nashville: "Recording proceeded at a furious pace, with five hundred sessions a year by 1958. That number would increase tenfold in the ensuing decade."

"How bad was it?" item four, from *Air Castle of the South*, Craig Havighurst's history of WSM radio: "Morale surged at the 1957 and 1958 [country music] DJ conventions. Country music seemed back on track."

"How bad was it?" item five, from Buddy Killen's autobiography: "Tree [publishing] had an excellent year in 1957."

Okay, so maybe 1957 wasn't so bad. Maybe it was even good. Fact is, in the late fifties, Nashville was busy becoming a major national recording center and by 1960 *Time* reported "Nashville has even nosed out Hollywood as the nation's second biggest (after New York) record-producing center."

There's a pesky little footnote. The records being made weren't necessarily country. "One out of every five popular hits of the past year was written and recorded in Nashville," reported *Time*. Of course, deciding what was pop and what was country in those days was a bit tricky.

"Since the spring of 1956, a country boy named Elvis Presley had been dominating both the pop and country charts," wrote Paul Kingsbury, onetime editor of *The Journal of Country Music*.

In 1955 both *Cashbox* and *Billboard* "picked him [Elvis] as the most promising new country and western artist," reported Craig Havighurst, and a 1956 article in *Billboard* held up Elvis as an example of "how country music is being accepted by the masses."

Elvis wasn't the only country act making noise on the pop charts. The Everly Brothers, Jerry Lee Lewis, Johnny Cash, and Don Gibson, among others, were going strong. (Even George Jones jumped on the bandwagon, recording rockabilly tunes under the name Thumper Jones.) So, for a while there, a lot of country music *was* rock 'n' roll. The numbers are overwhelming.

From 1956 through 1958, when rock 'n' roll was really getting going, eighty percent of *Billboard*'s number one country hits crossed over to the pop charts. Of those, nearly half reached the pop top five and about a third became number one. In 1957, Wesley Rose's so-called "disastrous" year, all but two of the fifteen number one country hits crossed over to the pop charts and the following year each and every one of the eleven number one country hits would make the jump.

So country, best-selling country anyway, *was* pop. Then somebody decided it wasn't. Who? Don't know for sure. But by the early sixties rock 'n' roll was all but gone from the country charts. Historian Diane Pecknold suspects a trio of Nashville heavyweights was responsible. According to the Nashville-based magazine *Music Reporter*, wrote Pecknold in *The Selling Sound: The Rise of the Country Music Industry*, in 1958 the Father, Son, and Holy Ghost of country music publishing—Jim Denny/Cedarwood, Jack Stapp/Tree, and Wesley Rose/Acuff-Rose—"went to New York and Los Angeles to hold 'personal pow-wows hoping to convince [*Variety* and *Billboard*] to eliminate rock 'n' roll from country and western charts.'"

Brent Olynick at Record Research Inc., the outfit that publishes all those reference books on the *Billboard* charts, denies it ever happened. "The decision was not 'Billboard's,'" he wrote me in an email.

Journalist Michael Kosser, in his book *How Nashville Became Music City U.S.A.*, blames the change on "country record promoters" who were demanding that "the trade magazines get the young rock 'n' rollers off the country charts before they destroyed the essence of country music." Country music deejays also may have had something to do with it, according to Pecknold, by offering "the most intense industry resistance to the new trend."

Whatever the particulars, the let's-kick-'em-off-the-charts crowd stormed the gates of the music establishment and, "by the end of 1961, Elvis and the Everly Brothers were gone from the country charts," reported Kosser. But the charts show little or no impact for Johnny Cash and Don Gibson.

I'll spare you the numbers, but the 1959–60 *Billboard* charts show Cash and Gibson actually got more, not less country play. Maybe somebody said, "We'll keep Cash and Gibson and give you Elvis and the Everly Brothers."

Yeah, sounds stupid to me, too.

Jerry Lee Lewis's country career did tank during this period. The Killer went from seven pop and six country charted records in 1957–58 to one pop and zero country charted records in 1959–60. But that's the kind of thing that can happen when you marry your thirteen-year-old cousin.

"I think that would be unusual anywhere except in our family," the girl's sister told the BBC years later. "My [other] sister was twelve when she got married. I was fourteen. We were very mature at a young age."

•   •   •

What we know so far: big, bad rock 'n' roll strutted into Nashville in the form of Elvis, the "hillbilly cat," around 1956 and five years later was escorted to the county line. Meanwhile, Nashville had become home to a big-time recording industry. So this whole notion that Nashville was under siege from rock 'n' roll is a crock. Far from killing country, "it was the success of rockabilly that finally established Nashville as the undisputed center of country music recording," wrote Diane Pecknold in *The Selling Sound*.

Still not convinced? By 1963 Nashville had "at least ten recording studios, ten talent agencies, four record pressing plants, at least twenty-six recording labels, and over two thousand musicians and performers," reported Joli Jensen in *The Nashville Sound*. More from Jensen: "This impressive industrial development took place during the time when country music's survival was allegedly at stake. . . . At a time when country music was supposedly barely surviving the onslaught of rock 'n' roll, Nashville was responding by developing an impressive system of country music oriented production, distribution, and marketing."

Later Jensen asked: "Why set up studios and talent agencies and music publishing houses in Nashville if country music is dead as a genre?"

Exactly.

But let's not let the facts get in the way of a good story. Let's see, where were we? Oh yeah, country music had to change or die. So beginning in the late fifties, Chet Atkins at RCA, the man Richard Peterson at Vanderbilt claimed was kicked off the Opry back in 1946 for playing jazz, and Decca's Owen Bradley, the leader of a big band called the Owen Bradley Orchestra, along with British import Don Law at Columbia and Anita Kerr, the vocal group leader and arranger extraordinaire of the Anita Kerr Singers, and Ken Nelson out at Capitol Records in California, in cahoots with a few others, all got together and conspired to silence the fiddles and steel, bring in the background vocals and the violins from hell, and, just like that, the great taste, less filling Nashville Sound, country music's answer to rock 'n' roll, was born.

Wrong. Wrong. Double wrong.

First off, thanks to Elvis, background vocals were firmly entrenched before the Nashville Sound era. As for country's loss of twang, blame Elvis again. He "almost single-handedly . . . rendered fiddles and steel guitars utterly passé in Nashville," wrote Paul Kingsbury, a one time editor of the *Journal of Country Music*. Then producers added the violins from hell to the mix and "the marriage of pop and country music was consummated," as Douglas Green and Bill Ivey put it in *The Illustrated History of Country Music*. But truth be told, pop-influenced country records were not new. Country and pop had been living in sin from the very beginning.

In the twenties, country's first star, singer Vernon Dalhart, he of "the rich, operatic stylings" as Vanderbilt's Richard Peterson put it, was a hit *before* down-home country fiddler Fiddlin' John

Carson and the Carter Family. In the thirties the most popular act on the Grand Ole Opry was not some string band, but the "smooth singing" Vagabonds, a trio of matinee-idol-handsome young men who performed in stylish business suits, according to *Country: the Music and the Musicians.*

"They could hardly be called 'country boys,'" the Opry's Judge Hay reportedly said of the group that sang what historian Robert Oermann called "Victorian parlor songs." In fact, before Roy Acuff came along to displace the Vagabonds in 1938, "the Opry seemed to be on a straight course toward becoming pop music," wrote Peterson.

Bite your tongue!

Then, following a salary dispute in 1946, Acuff himself was replaced as host of NBC radio's nationally broadcast Prince Albert segment of the Opry by future Country Music Hall of Famer Red Foley, "a folksy crooner" who sounded more like Eddy Arnold than Hank Williams. Foley is best remembered for hits "Chattanooga Shoe Shine Boy" and "Peace in the Valley." By 1955, in a move that anticipated the Nashville Sound era, Foley had swapped his cowboy garb for a business suit and was hosting *Jubilee U.S.A.* on ABC television.

That same year Eddy Arnold, who had been cutting pop-sounding ballads for years, created quite a stir when he ran off to New York—gasp!—and cut an uptown version of his 1945 recording of "Cattle Call" with the Hugo Winterhalter Orchestra. Talk about violins. At the time, wrote Diane Pecknold, the "string-laden, sweet pop arrangement by Hugo Winterhalter that anticipated the Nashville Sound, was as likely to face resistance [to air play from deejays] as a rockabilly hit."

This was the Nashville Sound several years before its official debut. (Robert Oermann has reported the term "Nashville Sound" first appeared in print in 1958 in *Music Reporter* and Patrick Carr says the "term [was] popularized by a 1960 *Time* magazine story.")

"As nearly as anybody can define it," reported *Time*, "the [Nashville] Sound is a byproduct of musical illiteracy." Because Nashville songwriters were unable to read music, reported *Time*, they "dream up new numbers by idly plucking a guitar until they stumble onto a tune."

Yeah, that's how it works.

As for that Nashville Sound conspiracy, the meeting where everybody got together and agreed to drop this and add that just to get the goat of purists of every stripe whether stone country devotee, folklorist, or deejay at some daytimer in northern Alabama? Never happened. The Nashville Sound was developed by trial and error, one record at a time.

"Maybe put strings on a record, and if that sells real well, then you do it again. And then you try some other background-voices, or harmonica, electric guitars in harmony, and you experiment around. And whatever sells, that's what you use," Chet Atkins told country music historian Alanna Nash.

"Whatever sells."

It took Owen Bradley several years to arrive at the Patsy Cline version of the Nashville Sound (first heard on "I Fall to Pieces" in 1961) during what Joli Jensen calls "an unfocused search for something that would work." Bradley tried all kinds of backgrounds, according to Jensen, who listened to every recording the two made together: Dixieland cornets, rock guitar, cocktail lounge piano, before settling on the background we've come to know and love/hate: the violins from hell and the Jordanaires. How did he know it worked? The records sold.

Here's how Chet Atkins described the trial and error process he used to launch the career of singer/songwriter Don Gibson in *Country: The Music and the Musicians*. Gibson's publisher, Wesley Rose of Acuff-Rose, told Atkins, "Let's keep it country."

"So we went in and made a session with fiddles and steel," recalled Atkins. "Didn't sell a one. And I said, 'Okay, let's do it my way this time, Wesley' . . . . So we got in the studio and did it my way [with no fiddles and steel] and, thank goodness, it was just a smash." Don Gibson's "Oh Lonesome Me" was number one for eight weeks in 1958.

Listen to the value system at work here. "Didn't sell a one." "It was just a smash." To Chet, records were good if they sold, bad if they didn't. Same goes for Owen. And if that meant drastic change, then, so the rationale went, "Country music had simply done what it had to do to save itself from rock 'n' roll," as Jensen phrased it.

So the name shouldn't have been the Nashville Sound. It should've been the That-Ain't-Sellin', So-Let's-Try-This Sound. Why make rock 'n' roll the bogeyman? To defend themselves from charges of selling out.

"The story of rock 'n' roll's onslaught allows a justification for change that is palatable to those who will never otherwise accept the genre's transformation," wrote Joli Jensen.

In other words, country music fans would be more likely to accept the violins from hell and background vocals if they thought they were necessary to save country music. But as Joli Jensen nicely put it [she's so damned polite]: "There are other ways to tell the story."

9

THE LONG, UNOFFICIAL, PRETTY-MUCH TOTALLY TRUE HISTORY OF THE NASHVILLE SOUND

When the Feds lifted the wartime freeze on radio licenses in 1945, the number of AM stations in the U.S. exploded from a little over nine hundred in 1945 to over twenty three hundred in 1952. (In those days, there were so few FM stations they weren't worth counting.) Before the expansion, ninety-five percent of stations were affiliated with one of the four national networks: NBC, CBS, ABC, and Mutual. But now there were a lot more stations than there were network slots. This led to the birth of a new force in broadcasting, the independents, who by 1952 accounted for just under half of all AM stations.

Without programming from the networks to rely on, the independents had to fend for themselves. At first most ended up running local versions of what was called block programming, a little of this and a little of that all day long. Here's what a typical day's schedule might have sounded like according to Marvin R. Benson at the University of Memphis:

> . . . lively "wake up music" in the AM, or country and western for the early-rising farmers and rural folks. Then mid-morning "pop" music or women's features. Around noon a news show and an hour of male-oriented programming might be run. The latest hits for teens came on around three PM when school let out. Then, a block of dinner music around five or six PM. Depending on how late the station was on, big band or jazz or R&B might fill the evening.

So stations programmed a little something for the whole family. Then came that dark and stormy night in 1949 or was it 1950 or 1951?

The name was Storz, Todd Storz. The blueblood son of an Omaha brewery owner, Todd had been a ham radio geek since he was a boy. Then in 1949, with a lot of help from his very rich daddy, the twenty-five-year-old bought an underperforming radio station, KOWH, from the *Omaha World-Herald* newspaper. Here's where the story gets good.

One night Storz and his program director, Bill Stewart, were having a few at a bar when Todd noticed something mighty peculiar. The clientele were playing the same song over and over and over again on the juke box. And then, even more peculiar, after closing time (it's not clear why our hero was still there after closing time), Todd spied a waitress feeding the juke box nickels so she could hear the exact same song the customers had been listening to over and over and over again all night long. And this wasn't the last time Todd would witness this phenomenon. "I saw waitresses do this time after time," said Storz. All this more or less according to Mark Fisher in his book *Something in the Air: Radio, Rock, and the Revolution That Shaped a Generation.*

Based on this irrefutable waitress evidence, so the story goes, Storz decided that all the thousands and thousands of people who listened to his radio station in Omaha were just like that waitress. They wanted to hear their favorite songs and they wanted to hear them over and over and over again. And if that was what they wanted, Todd was determined to give it to them. As he said years later, "If the public suddenly showed a preference for Chinese music, we would play it."

Soon a new radio format was born, one in which stations played listeners' favorite songs over and over and over again. It's called Top Forty.

Okay, that's the story of the birth of Top Forty radio you see everywhere, more or less. For those who find this oft-told account a bit on the fairy tale side, author Mark Fisher offers an alternative.

In this version, in 1950 a University of Omaha researcher is said to have given Storz a survey which showed that the people listening to his radio station preferred music shows and "wanted to hear their favorite songs over and over." Another version of the original juke box story, told by music writer Ben Fong-Torres, has Storz coming up with the idea before he even owned a station. "I became convinced that people demand their favorites over and over while in the Army during the Second World War," Storz reportedly told a 1957 interviewer.

Whenever and wherever he got his inspiration, wrote Fisher, Storz would end up canceling all the block programming on KOWH in Omaha: doing away with local offerings like Aunt Leana's homemaker show and the *Back to the Bible Hour*, and canceling the cheesy soap operas he had been "importing from England on jumbo-sized transcription discs." Then using the new format, Storz began playing nothing but music all day long. Now no matter what time of day listeners tuned in, they heard their favorite songs played over and over and over again.

"About the time you're ready to shoot yourself if you hear it one more time, it's hitting the Top Ten," a station manager once told his deejays.

The Top Forty formula worked. "By the end of 1951," wrote Fisher, "KOWH's share of Omaha listeners shot up from four to forty-five percent."

Ka-ching! Ka-ching!

Storz expanded to Kansas City, New Orleans, Minneapolis, and Miami, and "by 1956, the five Storz stations had gutted the ratings of well-established network affiliates," according to *Radio's Revolution*, a reelradio.com documentary.

As independent radio stations flourished, the national radio networks faded. According to a 1958 report from sales reps Adam Young Incorporated: "The top-rated radio stations in the nation's top twenty-five markets [cities] up to 1952 had been network affiliates. By 1957, the top-rated radio stations in twenty one of the top twenty five markets were independents, that is, non affiliates."

"The sole function served by radio networks is to provide coverage of national and international events," Top Forty pioneer Gordon McClendon told *Broadcasting* magazine in 1957. "In every other area of programming, local radio and or television is superior."

As early as 1952, local radio had put network radio in intensive care, claiming almost twice as much ad revenue. By the time television got up to speed in 1955, it was all over. That year's network TV revenue, about a half-a-billion dollars, was more than six times that of network radio. (All these stats are from *Stay Tuned: A History of American Broadcasting*.) Don't like numbers? Here it is in English. By the mid-fifties network radio was getting its butt kicked by both local radio and network TV. Soon network radio, the medium that had dominated American cultural life for more than a quarter of a century, was, as Jim Cox put it in *Say Goodnight, Gracie*, a "secondary entertainment source."

At best.

Meanwhile country music was also suffering at the hands of local radio. "A lot of stations that had block programming—blocks of time devoted to different kinds of shows," Jo Walker-Meador of the Country Music Association told Michael Kosser, "dropped country music in favor of shows featuring the top forty records in the country, regardless of genre."

Country was out. Top Forty was in. How in? Top Forty pioneer Bud Connell, a Storz disciple, said Top Forty was "so successful that by 1955 it had been copied coast to coast." But in *Stay Tuned: A History of American Broadcasting*, Christopher H. Sterling and John M. Kitross report that while there would be "hundreds" of Top Forty stations by 1960, there were only "about twenty" in 1955. Which is it? Not sure. There's no smoking gun here, but it looks like for a couple of years there, Top Forty buried country radio, but not with rock 'n' roll. In the early fifties when Top Forty was getting going, there was no rock 'n' roll. There was music programming modeled after *Your Hit Parade*, a top-ten countdown show that featured jewels like "If I Knew You Were Comin' I'd've Baked a Cake," number one for twelve weeks in 1950.

That was followed in 1951 by "Aba Daba Honeymoon," number two on "Your Hit Parade" for nine weeks.

Aba daba daba daba daba daba dab
Means "monk I love but you."

I call this junk "pop schlock"—and in the early days of Top Forty radio, it dominated the charts. I mean, it was grim. American popular music was going through a difficult, symphony-for-fingernails-on-blackboard, postwar period, and Top Forty pop schlock elbowed all other music programming off the air—country, big bands, jazz, R&B, you name it—and what was left was a one-size-fits-all Top Forty format aimed at teens. Why teens? Suddenly they were the ones buying all the records.

So it wasn't songs like "Hound Dog," A.K.A. the evil rock 'n' roll, that waylaid country music in the early fifties, but rather songs like "How Much Is That Doggie in the Window?," A.K.A. pop schlock. Not something new and raw and dangerous, but something old and syrupy and bland.

How much is that doggie in the window? (Arf! Arf!)
The one with the waggly tail.

"Doggie in the Window" was number one for eight weeks in 1953. After a few years of pop schlock just about anything would have sounded revolutionary. That "anything" turned out to be 1955's "Rock Around the Clock" by Bill Haley and the Comets.

"After being fed the aural equivalent of watercress for years, it didn't take the young ears of America long to recognize an entrée when it was served," wrote John Lomax III in *Nashville: Music City U.S.A.* "'Rock Around the Clock' was the first fresh-sounding music that mainstream radio had played in years. Eight months later Elvis's 'Heartbreak Hotel' hit number one and the sounds of American popular music changed forever."

But change didn't come across the board. Even during Elvis's peak years 1956–57, the pop schlock kept coming: stuff like number one hits "The Wayward Wind" by Gogi Grant (1956); Perry Como's "Hot Diggity (Dog Ziggity Boom)" (1956); and a series of ballads by Elvis's arch rival Pat Boone: "Don't Forbid Me," "Love Letters in the Sand," and "April Love," all in 1957.

Yes, I said "arch rival." From 1955 to 1959, there were two competing superstars running neck and neck for supremacy in the world of rock 'n' roll: Elvis Presley and Pat Boone. Boone was the clean-cut, church-going, parent-friendly face of rock. He had earned his rock 'n' roll stripes early in his career by recording sanitized cover versions of R&B songs "stolen" from the likes of Little Richard and Fats Domino. (No one could have been whiter than Boone or blacker than these two.) Boone hit the pop charts about a year before Elvis and had his first number one song eight months before the King with a cover of Fats Domino's "Ain't That a Shame." (Although he grew up in Nashville and was the son-in-law of Red Foley, Boone wouldn't make the country charts until 1975.)

Most of Boone's charted work after 1956 was sappy love ballads that had more in common with pop schlock than rock 'n' roll. But in his prime, the kids in my junior high school, at least, were taking sides. You were either in the Elvis camp or the Pat Boone camp. I remember giving this a lot of serious twelve-year-old thought (really), before ending up on the wrong side of history with Boone, the squeaky-clean, all-American boy.

So to recap: in the mid-fifties there was Elvis and there was Pat Boone, rock 'n' roll and pop schlock cohabitating on the pop charts, as rock 'n' roll and country were shacking up on the country charts. When rock 'n' roll was forced off the country charts, a vacuum was created. That vacuum was soon filled by an adult-oriented, pop-influenced music with a southern accent that came to be known as the Nashville Sound.

Let the marketing begin.

10

YEAH, BUT IS IT COUNTRY?

Modern country music has no relationship to rural or mountain
life. It is the music of this *Nation*, of this country, the music of the
people. You find no screech fiddles, no twangy guitars, no mournful nasal twangs in the *modern* Nashville sound of country music.
— RADIO CONSULTANT, circa 1958

The Country Music Association (CMA) was formed in 1958 out
of the remains of the Country Music Disc Jockeys Association
and then and now serves as kind of a trade association for the
business. Back in the early days, as Diane Pecknold reported in
The Selling Sound: The Rise of the Country Music Industry, the
CMA saw the country audience as "the rural to urban white
migrants from the South and Midwest who made up a significant
portion of the newly affluent blue-collar middle class."

Hillbillies made good.

In 1960, wrote Pecknold, the CMA mailed copies of a magazine article titled "Country Music: A Gold Mine for City Broadcasters" to three hundred advertising executives. The article
explained that the country audience "[was] not listeners who had
been lured away from the pop audience, but country music fans
who would not otherwise be reached by radio."

The CMA wanted to convince radio/ad executives that country music delivered a unique, hard-to-reach audience with money
to spend. In American broadcasting that's always a message with
some traction. Apparently it took. In 1961, according to a CMA
survey, there were only eighty-one stations playing country full-
time. Eight years later, there were over six hundred.

The Nashville Sound would prove to have staying power
despite "sticky sweet orchestral arrangements and mooing vocal

87

choruses," as Robert Palmer would put it in the *New York Times* decades later. Why? You know. It sold. And those who wanted to keep on driving those pink Cadillacs would soon adapt.

Listen to Chet.

"Somebody interviewing me once asked me, 'What's the Nashville Sound?,'" Atkins recalled in Nicholas Dawidoff's book *In the Country of Country*. "I was stumbling for an answer and he got out some coins and shook them and he was right. People were in it to make a living."

"What we did was we tried to make hit records," Chet continued. "We wanted to keep our job."

So was this selling out as some charged? Not if "selling out" means playing music you know is junk just to make a quick buck.

"For guitarist Atkins, a self-styled 'country gentleman' with a taste for classical music, and pianist Bradley, a society bandleader," wrote John Morthland in the *Journal of Country Music*, "this sound was a natural enough step in the evolution of the music."

"I was just making records I liked," Chet told historian Robert Oermann. "It turned out the public liked them too."

So if Chet and them didn't sell out, and rock 'n' roll didn't make Chet and them do it, then what was Chet and them's motive? Whence cometh the violins from hell? What's with the Nashville Sound? This time Chet and them's rationale rings true. They were trying to make hit records. The old formulas didn't work. They tried something new. When it sold, they copied each other. After the fact, somebody dubbed it the "Nashville Sound." The label stuck. When asked, they blamed it on the evil rock 'n' roll.

All done.

(I mean, no self-respecting country musician is ever going to admit to being done in by the likes of "Doggie in the Window.")

• • •

And here in the twenty-first century, decades after the debut of the Nashville Sound, what are we to make of all this pop-influenced country music?

"My first favorite, of course, was Roy Acuff," George told Sirius Radio deejay Charlie Monk in 2007. No surprise there. "And Eddy Arnold, of course, one of my favorites," continued George. "He was way ahead of his time 'cause he had such a smooth, good voice."

Eddy Arnold? Didn't Eddy Arnold abandon country music in the fifties? Don't you have to make a choice: Eddy or Roy? Can you really pick both?

Hello.

If George Jones, Mister Authenticity, the curator of curators, includes Eddy in the country club—pun intended—what are we to do but get down off our hardcore country high horse and give ole Eddy a welcome, tuxedo and all, along with Red Foley and Ray Price and, while we're at it, Patsy Cline and Jim Reeves who George also has given his belated approval.

"Well, she was pop," George thought when he first heard Patsy in the fifties. Sounded like "she oughta have an orchestra or something behind her." But as the years passed George came to appreciate both Patsy and Jim.

"I think Jim Reeves and Patsy Cline, especially, was way before their time," George told me.

"I can look back on it today and listen to Jim and her," he continued, "and I don't know why, I guess it's because I been in the same business, but today I can appreciate them so much more."

So it's settled, then. Like it or not, the Nashville Sound, this pop music with a southern accent, has been and will forever be classified as country music. All this despite the violins from hell. Maybe that's a good thing. The Nashville Sound opened things up for country music and in the end it was not about a particular sound, but a license to experiment that led to post–Nashville Sound classics like "He Stopped Loving Her Today" and "Stand By Your Man."

"In country music," singer-songwriter Mike Ireland told William Hogeland in the *New York Times* in 2005, "there's this suspicion of instrumentation. Other musics don't have it. Nobody goes, 'You know, those Al Green hits would really be great if you just took out the strings and singers.'"

"In Billy Sherrill's arrangements," wrote Hogeland in the same *Times* article, "a sobbing steel guitar can blend with, can be mistaken for, a soprano singer or one of the strings; at times it can be difficult to identify what instrument—marimba? harpsichord?—has been dubbed in."

"He's not just slopping stuff on the songs," Ireland told Hogeland, "but actually supporting almost line by line, what's going on emotionally. It's so nuanced."

And that never could have happened without the anything-goes climate created by the Nashville Sound. Sure, there were some really sappy records made, but like Beverley Keel of the *Tennessean* wrote, "good music eventually shines through because it cannot be denied. All the rest—the bubbly car candy and trendy unremarkable tunes—just fades to a blur."

Billy Sherrill with George Jones and Tammy Wynette in the studio. Nashville Public Library, Special Collections Division: *Nashville Banner* Archives.

March 10, 1956: Nashville Sound co-creator Owen Bradley (at piano) was equally at home with big bands and singers as diverse as Loretta Lynn and Patsy Cline. Nashville Public Library, Special Collections Division: *Nashville Banner* Archives.

March 10, 1971: Nashville nominees for 1970 Grammy Awards included Billy Sherrill (co-writer of "Stand by Your Man"), Brenda Lee (contemporary female vocalist), and Chet Atkins (instrumental performance). None of the three won. Photo by Bob Ray. Nashville Public Library, Special Collections Division: *Nashville Banner* Archives.

May 1971: Tammy Wynette and George Jones before their fairy-tale marriage fell apart. Nashville Public Library, Special Collections Division: *Nashville Banner* Archives.

January 10, 1975: Twenty-four hours after Epic shipped the Charlie Rich rendition of Curly Putman's "My Elusive Dreams" (co-written with Billy Sherrill), a profile of Putman appeared in the *Nashville Banner*. Nashville Public Library, Special Collections Division: *Nashville Banner* Archives.

November 14, 1975: About four months after their divorce, George and Tammy were still singing together. Photo by Don Foster. Nashville Public Library, Special Collections Division: *Nashville Banner* Archives.

October 13, 1977: Billy Sherrill with his wife Charlene and daughter Cathy at the 1977 BMI Awards banquet in Nashville. Photo by Bill Goodman. Nashville Public Library, Special Collections Division: *Nashville Banner* Archives.

March 10, 1978: Billy Sherrill at the keyboard in his office. Photo by Bill Goodman. Nashville Public Library, Special Collections Division: *Nashville Banner* Archives.

January 30, 1980: Exactly a week before he cut "He Stopped Loving Her Today" (if you believe the paperwork), George Jones came to Tammy Wynette's Nashville home to announce the two would once again record duets. Photo by Turner Hutchison. Nashville Public Library, Special Collections Division: *Nashville Banner* Archives.

June 13, 1980: As "He Stopped Loving Her Today" climbed the charts, fans mobbed George Jones at his Fan Fair booth in Nashville. Photo by Bill Goodman. Nashville Public Library, Special Collections Division: *Nashville Banner* Archives.

October 1981: Three of the greatest country music producers of all time, Billy Sherrill, Owen Bradley, and Larry Butler (Kenny Rogers), pose with Tree Publishing's Buddy Killen (second from right) in the early 1980s. Nashville Public Library, Special Collections Division: *Nashville Banner* Archives.

January 8, 1982: In early 1982, the *Nashville Banner* did a profile of songwriter Bobby Braddock. Photo by Bill Goodman. Nashville Public Library, Special Collections Division: *Nashville Banner* Archives.

May 1982: Curly Putman, CBS Executive Rick Blackburn, Bobby Braddock, Billy Sherrill, and Tree Publishing's Buddy Killen show off gold records in 1982. Nashville Public Library, Special Collections Division: *Nashville Banner* Archives.

June 3, 1982: George Jones and Tammy Wynette in 1982. Photo by Bill Goodman. Nashville Public Library, Special Collections Division: *Nashville Banner* Archives.

August 2, 1982: George Jones clowns around with Davidson County Sheriff Fate Thomas and pal Pee Wee Johnson. Photo by Bill Thorup. Nashville Public Library, Special Collections Division: *Nashville Banner* Archives.

September 27, 1993: Songwriter Bobby Braddock posed in front of a wall full of his awards in 1993. Nashville Public Library, Special Collections Division: *Nashville Banner* Archives.

PART FOUR

MUSIC MAKERS

FOLLOW THE MONEY

Oh they walk away from everything
Just to see a dream come true.
God bless the boys
That make the noise on Sixteenth Avenue.
—THOM SCHUYLER, "Sixteenth Avenue"

Early April, just another strip-mall, Hillsboro Road, Nashville, Tennessee. The nine o'clock show time was fast approaching and my songwriter friend Ellen Warshaw and I stood in a long, motionless line outside the Bluebird Cafe waiting to hear some of Nashville's premiere songwriters ply their trade. Forget the front porch, barnyard, and Blue Ridge mountain home, listening rooms like the Bluebird are where it really happens these days. Where an idea that came out of nowhere while taking a shower, mowing the lawn, or cruising aisle two at the nearby Green Hills Kroger—Dried Fruit, Rice, Jello—is heard out loud in public for the first time.

It was still sprinkling after a gray, rainy day and we were three awnings down from the entrance. From our vantage point it looked like there were too many people to fit into the tiny club. We were in the people-with-reservations line to the left of the door. To the right, there was a much shorter "hopefuls" line headed by a grumpy-looking, fiftyish guy sitting in a folding aluminum lawn chair.

A buxom young girl canvassed our line. "Reservations?" she asked.

"We have 'standing room' reservations," said Ellen. "Never heard of that," replied the girl.

Ellen nodded and continued chatting it up with a songwriter friend in line ahead of us. Ellen had played the Bluebird, knew how the place worked, so if she wasn't worried about us getting in, neither was I.

A transplanted New Yorker, Ellen is a rock singer turned songwriter (she had a record deal at age fifteen) who used to hang with pal Cyndi Lauper in the Big City. Now forty-something, she operates a bed and breakfast called The Big Bungalow over in East Nashville where she herself hosts an occasional writers' night.

This particular gathering of talent at the Bluebird was part of day three of Tin Pan South, Nashville's "annual celebration of song," as the *Tennessean* put it. This night alone, twenty big-time songwriters were scheduled to sit in circles swapping songs in simultaneous shows at six clubs including here at the sold-out Bluebird, where the headliner was Bobby Braddock, co-writer of "He Stopped Loving Her Today."

At nine the line finally began moving and just inside the door, Ellen queried the young Rubenesque woman at the counter.

"Jack Isenhour?"

"Jack Isenhour plus one," the woman replied, verifying our standing room reservations.

We shelled out seven dollars each for a ticket and the woman directed us to two stools just behind her counter. I sat on a round wooden stool, way too short to be a bar stool, more like a milking stool, directly behind her. It was close quarters and I had to be careful not to bump into the woman's blue-jeaned, Rubenesque bottom. But it was a lot better than standing for two hours.

I asked a guy who looked like he was in charge for a head count.

"We can hold a hundred," he said, looking around at the standing room only crowd. "But the fire code says seventy seven."

Seventy seven it is.

It was an intimate setting. The four songwriters were already set up in a circle in the center of the room surrounded by an audience seated at small tables. Nobody, including people in the bathroom, was more than about thirty feet from the performers. On the left was the bar and on the right a small stage, which would go unused. A big black-and-white banner hung on wall to the right of the stage: "N.S.A.I. welcomes you to Tin Pan South." N.S.A.I. is the Nashville Songwriters Association International, the sponsor of Tin Pan South, slogan: "It all begins with a song." And that slogan, whether you are talking art or business, gets at the heart of what's going on in this town. Whether a songwriter, singer, picker, publisher, or label executive, whether you call yourself an artist or a businessman, it's all about writing, recording, performing, and selling songs, songs, and more songs.

The lights dimmed, leaving small spotlights trained on the players. Bobby Braddock was on my left. He wore a black suit jacket and black crew neck pullover. He jabbed at his electronic keyboard—a big black and silver thing—generating a cheesy-on-purpose applause sample. Bobby reminded me of James Taylor, with a little bit more dark hair, a couple of day's growth of beard, and the same air of seriousness. Songwriter Matraca Berg ("Strawberry Wine") was seated to the right of Bobby, guitar in hand. A beautiful brunette, she was wearing a black top, jeans, and a diamond on the appropriate finger. Dean Dillon ("Tennessee Whiskey") sat to the right of Matraca, facing Bobby. This Tennessee boy's moustache and shoulder-length blond hair, along with the big, tan cowboy hat, made him look like Buffalo Bill.

I could only see the back of the fourth songwriter, Leslie Satcher, a pleasantly plump blonde in a sleeveless black top and jeans. She has had cuts by Reba, Vince Gill, George Strait, and Gretchen Wilson. Except for Bobby, all the writers were armed with guitars. The idea was to go around the circle, each writer taking turns singing a song they had written.

"I know that a song is done when I can play the whole thing in front of people and not wince at even one word," Nashville singer-songwriter Ashley Cleveland once told the *Tennessean*.

Bobby Braddock recognized Byrd Burton, formerly of the Amazing Rhythm Aces.

"Play your famous lick," said Bobby, and Burton played a guitar riff from "Third Rate Romance, Low Rent Rendezvous," before kicking in on Braddock's rendering of the Toby Keith hit "I Wanta Talk About Me" from 2001. The lyrics were so intricate that even Bobby had to read them. (Braddock calls it a rap song.) He finished one page, dropped it to floor, started another as my friend Ellen quietly sang along. Knew every word.

The song is a sentimental favorite for Braddock. It's the one that finally got him out of debt. At one point he owed a couple-hundred thousand to the IRS (taxes, fines, and penalties) and another couple-hundred thousand to his publisher (advances, advances, and more advances), Bobby told bankrate.com.

"I was in such terrible debt that I had to sell my writer's rights to my songs," Bobby continued. This was in the late eighties and it included the rights to "He Stopped Loving Her Today."

"If I had to do it over," said Braddock, "I would rather have lived in a little room and taken a bus to Music Row every day than to have given up my copyrights. That's a precious thing to let go of."

Even today Braddock says selling his rights "was the big-gest mistake I ever made in my life." Why? It will be costing him money until the day he dies. After that, it will be costing his heirs money.

"I'd like to play the one for you that bought the big-screen TV," said Leslie Satcher, and then sang the Martina McBride hit "When God-Fearing Women Get the Blues" from 2001. The gist: you'd best clear the area when love goes wrong for a "God-fear-ing" woman.

In her chitchat leading up to the song, Leslie confessed she came to Nashville wanting "to be Reba." She was so green at the time she didn't know you could actually make a living writing songs. Actually, it's easier to make money writing songs than singing them. Particularly over the long-term. That's because of the way royalties work. Time for Music Biz 101 where we do like an investigative reporter and "follow the money."

•   •   •

There are two basic kinds of royalties: mechanical and perfor-mance. Mechanical royalties are paid for the sale of a particular recording of a song whether a CD, tape, or download. Perfor-mance royalties are paid whenever a song is played out loud in public whether performed live or played back. (There are different wrinkles for movies, TV, operas, and Broadway musicals, but we're not going to fool with that.)

Here's the punch line: songwriters and publishers get paid both mechanical and performance royalties while singers are paid only mechanical royalties and then only eventually. Again, songwriters and publishers get paid royalties whenever a recording of their song is sold *or* the music is played out loud in public. Singers are paid royalties *only* when their particular recording of the song is sold. Eventually. Singers don't get paid anything because their hit single is being played, say, ten times a day on every country radio station in America. That's nuts and performers have tried to get it fixed for years. No luck so far. There is some hope. Legislation has been passed that could end up giving singers significant performance royalties for songs heard on line.

Meanwhile, the royalties the singers do collect from the sales of recordings are slow in coming. While songwriters and publishers are paid their cut of these mechanical royalties off the top, singers don't get a nickel until the label makes back— "recoups"—every cent it has invested in the singer: things like an advance, the costs of recording, marketing, music videos, and those hotel accommodations at the Bellagio in Vegas for the label exec who showed up unannounced to provide "moral support." This means it's going to be awhile before you, the singer, see any royalty money. A bunch of hit records down the line when you get to be a big, big star, the royalties will come, in torrents. But for now, enjoy that gigantomongous billboard with your picture on it at the Broadway/West End Avenue split in Nashville. You paid for it.

A couple of years into a successful career, singers often end up feeling like they're paying the label instead of the label paying them. That's because they are. From the label's point of view, the singer is paying back a loan. From the singer's point of view, the labels are robber barons who use "unconscionable contracts and corrupt accounting tactics to rob artists of their share of earnings," as reporter Chuck Philips summarized the singers' side of the argument in the *Los Angeles Times*.

"If we're not songwriters, and not hugely successful commercially (as in platinum [million]-plus), we [recording artists] don't make a dime off our recordings," said singer-songwriter Janis Ian.

Back in 2001, Courtney Love raised a ruckus on behalf of her fellow recording artists claiming they were being paid "royalties that represent a tiny fraction of the money their work earns." She had horror stories.

Toni Braxton and other multi-platinum artists "have been forced to declare bankruptcy," Love wrote in her "Letter to Recording Artists." Florence Ballard from the Supremes "was on welfare when she died," Love continued, and, closer to home, Merle Haggard, who had thirty-seven number one country singles in the twentieth century, "never received a royalty check" until the twenty-first.

Then there's George Jones. "I kept going to different labels, thinking I'd find one that paid me," George told an interviewer. "But I never did."

There is a way out.

"If you are merely the recording artist or hit-making producer, but want a taste of that performance royalty money from radio airplay, you must acquire some of the credit for writing or publishing," wrote singer-songwriter Joel Mabus.

Colonel Tom Parker was all over this one. To get Elvis to record a song, a songwriter with no clout had to give Elvis a piece of the action. So when it came time to divvy up the proceeds, Elvis was listed not only as the singer, but as the co-writer and, at times, even the publisher of a song.

Mind you, this had nothing to do with Elvis wanting to steal creative credit from songwriters like Otis Blackwell, famously ("Don't Be Cruel," "All Shook Up"), or anybody else. This was strictly a business deal. "I've never written a song in my life," Elvis freely admitted. (This according to biographer Peter Guralnick in *Last Train to Memphis*.)

It was all about money, honey.

"If Presley published the song and recorded it, he was paid twice every time a record sold; and if he got a co-writing credit, he was paid three times, and so was Parker who set it all up," explained Donald Clarke in *The Rise and Fall of Popular Music*.

So how much money are we talking about? Circa 2006, a million-selling song would generate about ninety thousand dollars in mechanical royalties for the songwriter and publisher to split, wrote Jason Blume in *This Business of Songwriting*. Singers' mechanical royalties are calculated separately. Singers get whatever percentage of the "suggested retail price" they negotiated when they signed with the label. Newcomers get about eight percent, stars a lot more. (Of course, this being the music biz, nobody *really* gets eight or fifteen or twenty percent. Ask your lawyer for details.)

Meanwhile, performance royalties for a number one country song during the "first year of release" will be somewhere between six hundred thousand and a million dollars, according to Blume in 2006. So called "performance rights societies" (ASCAP, BMI, and SESAC, mostly) keep up with who plays what, when; collect fees; and pay royalties directly to songwriters and publishers.

Some advice for singers waiting around for their mechanical royalties to start rolling in: patience, your time is coming. Once you prove you can make money, then you can stick it to the label and listen to *them* whine.

"About six seconds before they go back into the studio to record the follow-up, you get the gun to your head," one label chief complained to reporter Chuck Phillips of the *Los Angeles Times*. "We call it 'the second album hold-up.' They want bigger advances. They want better royalties."

Don't we all. And we would want those "bigger advances!" and "better royalties!" even if the labels hadn't been holding us up. The Dixie Chicks certainly felt they were getting robbed by Sony a few years back. The Chicks had sold twenty million albums, reported *Time*, and the group claimed Sony "had made two hundred million off of them," while they individually hadn't cleared their first million. Not that the label's two hundred mil was pure profit. The Chicks were helping pick up the tab for the other acts Sony invested in that failed. Across the industry, that's about nine out of every ten new acts signed.

"Every new act signs a bad deal," said Dixie Chick fiddler Martie Maguire, waxing philosophical in *Time*.

The Chicks sued, charging "systematic thievery," reported the *New York Times*, and about the time the folks who just fell off the turnip truck (my hand *is* raised) thought something might really change, the Chicks settled legally and figuratively. Sold out. And who can fault them? According to *Entertainment Weekly*, Sony gave them their own label (Open Wide Records—not gonna touch that one), jacked up their royalty rate to twenty percent, and advanced them twenty million dollars.

That's a two and—count 'em—seven zeros. Oh, one little thing: fifteen million dollars of that advance? Recouped by Sony, said *Entertainment Weekly*, to pay "marketing costs."

And what of Courtney Love, the woman on the white horse come to rescue the Godly artists from the demonic record labels? She too settled, reportedly receiving a four-million-dollar advance.

Tsk tsk, said the *New York Times*.

"Ms. Love joins numerous other artists who have sued record labels, saying that they want to expose and change unfavorable industry practices, but ended up settling for personal gain," wrote Neil Strauss.

That seems a little harsh. Granted, Courtney's original idea was to stop what the Chicks called "systematic thievery" throughout the music biz and not just in her own little opium den, but still, in the end, wasn't "personal gain" what her lawsuit was all about in the first place?

I thought so.

A footnote: amazingly, session musicians don't get paid any royalties at all. No mechanical royalties when a recording is sold. No performance royalties when a recording is played. Instead these musicians get paid a flat rate for working a session and then, greatly simplifying here, are cut an annual check based on what percentage their work represents of all the session work done in the U.S. that year. The more you work, the more you're paid. And while your percentage of the whole will be very, very small, the pot is very, very big.

"I used to get checks at the end of the year that would choke a mule," said drummer Jerry Carrigan. "I mean big amounts of money. Big. Big. Big. Five figures."

This mad money comes from something called the Sound Recording Special Payments Fund which is financed by the record labels (based on sales) and managed by the American Federation of Musicians—the union.

"My biggest check, I don't mind telling you, I got thirty-four-thousand dollars one year," said standup bass player Bob Moore.

And that was decades ago. All this helps explain why Bob Moore "went twelve years without even one day off," and Charlie McCoy "was in the studio day and night."

12

THE WRITING OF "HE STOPPED LOVING HER TODAY"

Back at the Bluebird, the music continued as a pretty young woman in a good-God-almighty, it's-spring! turquoise dress cozied up to guest songwriter Gary Nicholson. "Honey can you squeeze me in," she sang, dishwater blonde hair spilling over the microphone.

Suddenly the rain hammered on the plate glass windows, and heads turned, as a Tennessee "gully washer" blew through. Dean Dillon called a reluctant Paul Overstreet ("Same Ole Me") up out of the audience. He sat to the left of Dillon in Matraca Berg's seat, borrowed her guitar. Overstreet was wearing a cowboy hat that looked to be white straw, a denim shirt, and jeans. A narrow, neatly trimmed beard followed his jaw line.

"Play my favorite song," said Leslie Satcher.

Overstreet hit a lick, sang, "I think she only loves me for my willie."

"Not that! That's nasty," said Leslie.

At 10:30, Bobby Braddock started the last round with—what else?—"He Stopped Loving Her Today." By chance, this came on the first day I'd heard anybody other than George Jones perform the song. That afternoon I'd listened on line to renditions by Johnny Cash, pianist Floyd Cramer, and the rock group Hammerlock, among others. Now Bobby Braddock. Based on that sampling, the news was grim. It was not only hard to figure why anyone would choose "He Stopped Loving Her Today" as the best country song of all time, it was hard to figure why anyone would have recorded it in the first place.

Later I asked Bobby for a copy of the demo hoping it would provide a clue. Didn't.

"A pretty paltry demo, really, compared to the great record they cut," admitted Braddock.

"I sang it and stacked instruments," he recalled. "I had a Moog synthesizer—bass, a string machine, electric piano—and the engineer [Eddy Anderson] played drums on it."

There also was some guitar in there and something that sounded like a touch of steel.

As for lyrics, "He Stopped Loving Her Today" was not one of these tunes that was dashed off on the back of a Krispy Kreme napkin in fifteen minutes. Bobby first made mention of the song in his journal on March 4, 1977. "Curly and I wrote half of 'He Stopped Loving Her Today,'" it read. The next surviving mention (some of the journal is missing) came more than seven months later, on October 18, 1977, when Braddock noted that he and Curly had finished "what we started, 'He Stopped Loving Her Today.'" Not that anybody much cared. Both Bobby and his publisher were more excited about a song written about the same time titled "When One Falls Out and One Stays In."

Not even the recording of the demo on October 20, 1977, would put an end to the writing of "He Stopped Loving Her Today." That particular set of lyrics would turn out to be little more than a first draft of the version eventually recorded by George Jones.

"The original form of the song was considerably different from what they ended up with," recalled Bobby.

Specifically, the original lyrics were tweaked throughout, Bobby and co-writer Curly Putman wrote another four lines that became the recitation, and stuff was moved around because of the sensitive subject matter. When you're dealing with death, said Curly, "You just can't come out and flat out say it in a song." You have to be subtle about it. And Curly would know. But let's start at the beginning.

•   •   •

"Curly always said I brought the idea to him," recalled Bobby Braddock.

Again, this was in 1977. At the time, Curly Putman was a song plugger, "writer relations guy," and unofficial song doctor at Tree Publishing.

"I remember sitting down and going over it for a few hours," Bobby said. "We did a lot of dark humor stuff. I remember funeral jokes like, 'if you think he looks good now [dead], you should have seen him a week ago.'"

Curly remembered it a little differently. He recalled Bobby bringing in more than just an idea. "He had the song, the idea started," said Curly.

"I was more of a consultant," he added later.

This was not the first time the two had worked together. Notably, about a decade earlier, Bobby had brought "D-I-V-O-R-C-E" to doctor Putman for treatment. (That classic song is about divorcing parents who spell out the "D word" so their four-year-old son won't know what they're up to.)

"I asked Curly, I said, 'Why has nobody recorded this song?' He said, 'I think the melody is a little too happy for such a sad song.' And I said, 'What would you do?' And it was basically around one line: 'I wish we could stop this D-I-V-O-R-C-E.' What I had, it sounded kind of like a soap commercial and Curly just 'saddened it up.'"

To be exact, Bobby told *Black and White*, a Birmingham weekly, "he [Curly] sang this real mournful sounding thing and I said, 'God, let's get this on tape.' I took it to Billy Sherrill and he cut it right away."

It was Sherrill and Tammy Wynette, of course, who turned the song into a country classic in 1968.

"Geographically speaking," said Bobby, "it was small help, but it made the difference in the song becoming recorded, becoming a standard."

(Did you write "D-I-V-O-R-C-E" with Tammy in mind?)

"No. Not at all," replied Bobby. "It was not necessarily thought of as a female song."

• • •

"So who wrote what?" I asked Curly, when the two songwriters were cranking out "He Stopped Loving Her Today," Curly writing on his guitar, Bobby on the "little ole electric keyboard" in Curly's office at Tree Publishing on Music Row.

("He had underlined in red every single 'I Love You'"?)

"Bobby," said Curly.

("First time I'd seen him smile in years"?)

"That's Bobby," said Curly. "You're trying to really put me down. You know, I could lie about this."

("This time, he's over her for good.")

"Uh, can't remember," said Curly.

"Do me a favor," Curly said five minutes later. "Ask Bobby those three questions."

Never did. That's because I figured Curly probably had it about right. While he would get a bigger cut of the song following the final rewrites, the initial contract gave Bobby seventy-five and Curly twenty-five percent of the royalties.

So why exactly did Bobby bring the song to Curly in the first place? Curly thinks it was because he had experience writing about death.

"There could be something to that," Bobby said.

"They always told me that I could kill 'em off pretty easy in songs cause of 'Green, Green Grass of Home,'" said Curly.

Knowing how to handle death is a handy skill in country music. It is such a common topic that Charles Reagan Wilson at the University of Mississippi came up with six categories of death in his essay "Digging Up Bones: Death in Country Music," including "violent and tragic death," "death and the family," and "celebrity death."

Then there's death by execution.

Until talking to Curly, I'd always thought "Green, Green Grass of Home" was this happy-go-lucky, Tom Jones piece about a simple homecoming where a guy was met by his "Mama and Papa" and a girlfriend with "hair of gold and lips like cherries." Come to find out all that happy stuff was a dream. The guy actually came home in a pine box, courtesy of the state, And once he got there, they laid him 'neath [as in underneath] the green, green grass of home.

Bummer.

"My Elusive Dreams" is another Putman tune that deals with death. That's the song about the restless couple who can't get it together.

You followed me to Texas.
You followed me to Utah.
We didn't find it there
So we moved on.

Did you know the clueless twosome lose their only child in the third verse? ("This time only two of us moved on.") Me neither. Curly was so subtle (with the help of co-writer Billy Sherrill) that it went right over my head.

Compared to "Green, Green Grass of Home" and "My Elusive Dreams," "He Stopped Loving Her Today" is direct. There are two phrases in the song, both in the chorus, that establish without a doubt that the man is dead: "They placed a wreath upon his door" and "Soon they'll carry him away." Are these the work of death merchant Curly? That's lost to memory. But whoever wrote what, when they were through nobody was falling all over themselves trying to record the song.

"It was probably a year before we ever got it, had it cut," said Curly. And then by Johnny Russell, who "recorded it twice for two different labels," recalled Braddock. Nothing happened, but song plugger Dan Wilson from Tree didn't give up on the song. He brought it to über producer Billy Sherrill.

"I thought it was a fantastic idea, but it wasn't written quite right," recalled Sherrill. "I thought the idea was like one of a kind, especially those great lines in there, like 'He had underlined in red every single "I love you"'. . . 'First time I'd seen him smile in years.' That's the one I had to go in the next room and put on an overcoat to keep from freezing to death."

"Billy called us and asked us to rewrite it," Braddock told Bob Allen in *George Jones: The Life and Times of a Honky Tonk Legend.* "We showed him another version that we'd already written for Johnny Russell, but he didn't like that version either. So we rewrote it again, and he still wasn't satisfied."

What was he looking for?

"Billy Sherrill wanted us to expand on it and write this verse about the woman returning after the husband or boyfriend passed away," recalled Braddock.

"Curly tells me we had initially written a verse like that and discarded it," Bobby continued.

"We were having her standing, maybe in the background," recalled Putman.

Curly and Bobby reworked the verse. They showed it to Billy. They were on the right track, but he still wasn't satisfied. So they reworked it again.

"They worked on it and worked on it," recalled Sherrill. "But I was a little harder to satisfy than them. They wanted a record. I wanted a hit. I wanted a standard."

"This went on for about a half dozen rewrites until finally he called us back and told us, 'That's it! You got it!'" Bobby told Bob Allen. The new verse:

You know she came to see him one last time.
Oh and we all wondered if she would.
And it kept running through my mind,
This time he's over her for good.

Years later George told an interviewer he had written an "almost identical" verse. "It's funny how you think together," he said.

"If he wrote it, I never heard it," said Sherrill. "The only thing besides his great performance, finally, the only thing Jones contributed in the seminal stages of the record was singin' it like 'Help Me Make It Through the Night' (laugh)."

Once the rewrite was complete, Bobby thought Curly deserved more credit. "I said, 'Curly, you certainly earned more than twenty-five percent on this,'" recalled Braddock. "So he said, 'Oh, okay. I'll take one third then.' That's how we left it."

"If we had to do it over again," continued Bobby, "I'd split it down the middle with Curly. I mean, if not for Curly, the song wouldn't have been written."

With the new verse, Sherrill was almost done. But there was still an issue with the chorus. "I wanted to wait to the bitter end to show he died," said Sherrill.

"It kept naggin' me that they got it over with too quick," he continued. "Like thirty seconds into the song and then the rest of it is just anticlimactic."

"I called Braddock and Curly and said, 'You killed this guy off too quickly, y'know. All the suspense is gone. You need to string it out toward the end of the record before the guy dies," recalled Sherrill.

When all was said and done, Sherrill wouldn't need the services of Braddock and Curly to "string it out." He simply moved the chorus so it wasn't heard until after the second verse.

"That breaks a cardinal rule," said Braddock. "You're supposed to get right down to the basic idea earlier in the song. A person would have had to have waited a minute, forty-five seconds before they even knew the song had to do with death."

"So that record had to be compelling enough to hold people's attention to that point," continued Braddock.

Moving the chorus was the last in a series of changes to the demo. For the record, here are all the revisions verse by verse. I'll give you the changes, then the finished verse. (You may want to fast forward through this.)

In the first verse, "*But as time* went slowly by" became "*As the years* went slowly by;" "*the* wall" became "*his* wall;" and there was a "but" dropped from the beginning of the next to last line.

> He said I'll love you 'til I die.
> She told him you'll forget in time.
> ~~BUT AS TIME~~ As the years went slowly by,
> She still preyed upon his mind.
>
> He kept her picture on ~~THE~~ his wall.
> Went half crazy now and then.
> ~~BUT~~ He still loved her through it all
> Hoping she'd come back again.

In the first half of the second verse, "*They found* some letters by the bed," became "*Kept* some letters by the bed," keeping the point of view consistent throughout the verse.

> ~~THEY FOUND~~ Kept some letters by the bed
> Dated nineteen sixty two.
> He had underlined in red
> Every single "I love you."

The point of view for most of the song is what's called third-person omniscient (the story is being told by a narrator who, like God, knows what everybody is thinking). The exception is the second half of the second verse, where the use of "I" signals the point of view has switched to first person.

> *I* went to see him just today.
> Oh but *I* didn't see no tears.
> All dressed up to go away.
> First time *I'd* seen him smile in years.

Glad that's over.

More lyric changes (still in the second verse): "I went to see him *one last time*" became "I went to see him *just today*," making it more immediate, like a newscast. Still in the second verse, "But I didn't *shed* no tears," became "I didn't *see* no tears," making the focus the tearless dead man rather than the narrator; and "He was really looking fine" became "All dressed up to go away" to maintain (and improve upon) the rhyme scheme. More on that in a second.

> I went to see him ~~ONE LAST TIME~~ just today.
> Oh but I didn't ~~SHED~~ see no tears.
> ~~HE WAS REALLY LOOKING FINE~~ All dressed up to
>   go away
> First time I'd seen him smile in years.

As for that double negative—"Oh but I didn't see *no* tears"— it survived every rewrite, a not so subtle reminder that this was, after all, a *country* song.

In the chorus, "*Tomorrow* they'll carry him away" became "*And soon* they'll carry him away," again making the time reference more immediate.

> He stopped loving her today.
> They placed a wreath upon his door.
> ~~TOMORROW~~ And soon they'll carry him away.
> He stopped loving her today.

Finally there was the new spoken verse devoted to the woman's return.

> You know she came to see him one last time.
> Oh and we all wondered if she would.
> And it kept running through my mind,
> This time he's over her for good.

Although it doesn't even rise to the trivia level of the point-of-view discussion above, the rhyme scheme for the verses is ABAB. That means the last word in the first line rhymes with the last word in the third line and the last word in the second line rhymes with the last word of the fourth line.

Or not.

While "time" and "mind" from both the first verse and the new verse come close to rhyming, they really don't.

> He said I'll love you 'til I die.
> She told him you'll forget in *time*.
> As the years sent slowly by,
> She still preyed upon his *mind*.

The chorus has a different rhyme scheme: ABAA. "Today" in the first line rhymes with "away" in the third and "today" in the fourth.

> He stopped loving her *today*.
> They placed a wreath upon his door.
> Soon they'll carry him *away*.
> He stopped loving her *today*.

At the time the song was recorded, Sherrill was producing a whole stable of artists for CBS. Why was this a George Jones song?

"I don't know. I just couldn't envision anybody singin' it but him probably," said Sherrill. "Paycheck could have done it. Paycheck could have done it real well. Merle Haggard could have done it. But Paycheck was out of the picture and Haggard was on another label. He [George] was the only one around I figured could really give a reading on that song that'd make you believe it. I couldn't imagine Charlie Rich singin' it."

So the historic decision was made: Billy Sherrill would produce George Jones on "He Stopped Loving Her Today." And with that, the soon-to-be classic song was on its way to the recording studio.

• • •

It was close to eleven and Ellen and I were already out the door of the Bluebird when writer Jon Randall was called up out of the audience. Ellen rushed back in to claim her stool. I had already lit up, and, choosing nicotine over art, sidled up to the speaker outside, watching through the window as Randall sang his then current hit, "Whiskey Lullaby."

You know the song. It's the one about a pair of lovers' double suicide featuring the bone-chilling line: "He put the bottle to his head and pulled the trigger."

That song.

Later, as Ellen and I walked along the sidewalk headed to our cars, she talked about how the lyrics to "Whiskey Lullaby" had been rewritten. In the original, she said, the instant-classic line, "He put the bottle to his head and pulled the trigger," was followed by "And finally *blew* away her memory." In the rewrite, said Ellen, it became "And finally *drank* away her memory."

Better. Less graphic. More subtle. More retro. More Curly. Still the old pros worry.

"Now, if we wrote 'He Stopped Loving Her Today,' I don't know if you could get someone to cut it," Curly told me.

Maybe not. But Brad Paisley and Alison Krauss—two big, mainstream country stars—*did* cut "Whiskey Lullaby," and the song *did* get nominated for CMA song of year, and the song *does* tap into the same vein, the same country music tradition, that spawned "He Stopped Loving Her Today" more than a generation ago.

"The song of unrequited love has long been a staple in country music," wrote Charles Reagan Wilson in his essay on death in country music; and, of course, we have always been able to count on country songwriters pushing that particular idea to its tee-total limit. Take "Little Darlin' Pal of Mine," the old Carter Family tune.

> Just three things that I wish for.
> It's my casket, shroud, and grave.
> When I'm gone, don't weep for me.
> Just kiss those lips that you betrayed.

(How's about I just blow you one from across the room?)

So much for subtlety. From the beginning, country songwriters have taken their love (and death) very, very seriously. "Many a suffering narrator seemed to believe that only death could quiet a broken-hearted lover," as Charles Reagan Wilson put it.

So we have the guy in "He Stopped Loving Her Today" saying "I'll love you 'til I die" and the guy in "Whisky Lullaby" writing "I'll love her 'til I die" in his suicide note and both being as good as their word.

(It's true love, I tell you.)

"The character in the song, incidentally, I think is a very bad role model," Bobby Braddock said of the jilted lover in "He Stopped Loving Her Today" in *News and Views*, the magazine of the National Music Publishers' Association.

"He should just have moved on. It makes for a good story song, but it's certainly no way to go about living your life."

(To be continued.)

13

THE QUONSET HUT

Music Row's ground zero.
—MICHAEL KOSSER

No question, that's hallowed ground.
—KYLE YOUNG, Director, Country Music Hall of Fame and Museum

In the mid-fifties, Owen Bradley converted the basement and most of first floor of a two-story brick house at 804 Sixteenth Avenue South into the first recording studio on what would become Nashville's Music Row. Outside, its original columns removed, front porch reconfigured, the finished building was fainting-architect ugly, but inside, it worked.

"We recorded down in that basement a lot. We did Burl Ives records down there," recalled background singer Millie Kirkham.

About a year after it opened, the facility they called Bradley's Film and Recording Studio got even uglier when a military-surplus, World War II–era, prefabricated metal building called a quonset hut was thrown up in the backyard. The addition looked like a gigantic, half-buried pipe and measured thirty-five feet high and seventy-eight feet long. Little filming of note ever went on in what was called Studio B, but Bradley did record landmark records there with the likes of Patsy Cline, Brenda Lee, Loretta Lynn, Kitty Wells, and Ernest Tubb.

Bradley sold the Quonset Hut to CBS in 1962 and a few years later his creative heir, Billy Sherrill, took over the place and would add David Houston, Charlie Rich, Tammy Wynette, Johnny Paycheck, Tanya Tucker, and, of course, George Jones to the lineup of stars who recorded in the building. Kris Kristofferson was around, too. Not singing, sweeping. He got his start as a CBS janitor.

If you believe the eyewitnesses, not the paperwork (we'll sort that out later), the first recording session for "He Stopped Loving Her Today," took place in the Quonset Hut sometime in late 1978 or early 1979. No one is one hundred percent sure exactly who was there at that first go-around, but Bob Moore (drummer Jerry Carrigan dubbed him "the king of the hillbilly bass players") is high on the list of usual suspects.

"We used to call him 'the bulldozer,'" Carrigan said. "Man, he'd get that tempo in that head and he'd bulldoze you through."

A session musician's session musician, Moore was a charter member of the A Team, the pioneering group that helped the Nashville recording industry blossom in the fifties.

"There was no other bass players around at that time that could do what I could do. Even at sixteen," said Moore. "That's not being immodest. That's being truthful."

In the fifties, Moore would record with some familiar names—"I was doin' Elvis and I was doin' Jerry Lee"—and whoever else came through town. By the time the recording session for "He Stopped Loving Her Today" rolled around, Moore, then in his late forties, had played on records that sold millions and millions and millions of copies. As for "He Stopped Loving Her Today": "I don't remember the day and the record session and when we did the song or anything about anything that happened while we were doing the song," said Moore.

Neither does George Jones.

"There have been so many [recording sessions] at this point in my career that they seem interchangeable," wrote George in his autobiography.

This "studio amnesia" is a common affliction, according to Moore's wife Kitra. "The musicians have an automatic clearing process in their brain," she said, so they can start fresh every day. This means many, like Bob, don't remember much of anything.

Then there's Charlie McCoy.

"I remember it exactly," said harmonica player McCoy of the first session for "He Stopped Loving Her Today." "I know where I was standing."

McCoy was an old pro by the time he cut the classic tune. After migrating to Nashville from Miami in 1961, where he played stand-up bass in his high school "orchestra" and spent some time at the University of Miami, Charlie McCoy would become Nashville's premiere session harmonica player.

"It was something I could do that no one else here was doing," said McCoy.

The first session he ever saw was with teen phenom Brenda Lee. The first session he ever played on was for the surname-challenged Hollywood sexpot Ann-Margret, a starlet even more lacking in, let's call it "subtlety," than her fellow Elvis consorts. That was in 1961. The very same week McCoy would play on a Roy Orbison session. It was a flashy beginning for a long career. "I had a string of fifteen consecutive years that I did more than four hundred sessions a year," said McCoy.

McCoy would go on to become the musical director of *Hee Haw* for eighteen of that show's twenty-four-year run. While the comedy was corny by design, "when we did the music on *Hee Haw*," said McCoy, "it was well done." And that was his day job when Sherrill assistant Emily Mitchell asked him to come in for the "He Stopped Loving Her Today" session.

"The band, George, and the vocal group was there," said McCoy. "I think they overdubbed the strings. But everybody else was there."

Coming in through the Quonset Hut's alley-side door, McCoy walked past the control room on the immediate left. This was Sherrill's headquarters, a soundproof booth with a giant sound mixing board, a half dozen or so tape recorders, and a big picture window so Sherrill could see everything that was going on.

"As you came in from the back, you walked down through the studio, down to the end, the drums and bass player were over against the wall [on the far right]," recalled McCoy. "The piano was right beside them [on the left]. The rhythm guitar player was like down at the end of the piano right by the drummer." A second acoustic guitar player sat close by. To the left of them, the lead guitar player sat by "a table there where he put the amplifier." The steel guitar player sat next to that same table.

"If you were in the control room looking out, continued McCoy, "you'd see the back of the singer and then beyond him would be the group of musicians. And then to the left of the singer would be the background singers. And to the right of the singer was a little alcove there—that's where I was."

The session began as always with producer Billy Sherrill coming out into the studio to go over the song with the pickers.

"You just get in there and kinda let 'em start runnin' it down and tell them, kinda what you want to do. 'You lay out here,'" said Sherrill. 'You come in here. You don't play at all. You don't play 'til the second chorus 'cause [there's] too much going on up front' and all that. And they're so good, they know just about what to do every time."

As they went over the song, acoustic guitar player Pete Wade scribbled down a chart using the famous Nashville chord numbering system invented by the Jordanaires. Meanwhile, Charlie McCoy was biding his time.

"They were running the song down and I was just waiting because with Billy Sherrill, you always kinda got specific instructions," said McCoy. "That's the way he was. And so I was waiting."

Old-school producers like Sherrill were session Nazis. They picked the songs to be sung, the musicians who would play them, and the studio where they would be recorded. The country prototype? Owen Bradley.

"When they say 'Owen Bradley,' they also say 'Chet,' and it wasn't that way," said Bob Moore.

(So Owen was the dude?)

"Uh huh. The *man*."

Bradley was a major influence on Billy Sherrill.

"I stole so much from Owen Bradley that I feel like Willie Sutton [the notorious bank robber]," said Sherrill.

"He was a very, very cool customer, I guarantee you that. Very, very cool," said Charlie McCoy.

"Owen Bradley made records fifty years ago that sound like they were made last night. He just had this knack, knowing how to make records," said Sherrill.

A local boy made good, Bradley first played trombone in dance bands at bordering-on-sleazy clubs on the outskirts of Nashville. He then moved up to big bands—orchestras—for the country club set while always keeping his radio day jobs, first at WLAC and then at WSM where he was a staff pianist and later bandleader. In the mid-fifties, after eighteen years at WSM, Bradley went out on his own as a studio owner/Decca record producer.

"He was a complete music man," said McCoy. "Never any problems. You went into one of his sessions, it was really run well. Billy Sherrill was the same way. He was a hands-on kind of guy whereas Chet and some of the guys . . . were kind of, y'know, let the musicians go and see what they can come up with. . . . Owen and Billy both went in with pretty specific ideas of how they were approaching things."

Chet? He knew how to delegate.

"Owen was out there with hands-on production. Owen knew what he was doin'. But if it was Chet, he was sittin' there in the control room readin' a magazine or had his guitar practicing and had the speakers turned off," said Moore. "They say, 'Well that's just a different style of producing.' Uh, actually there's a lot of truth in that. A big part of producing is helping pick the songs out that you're gonna do. And that's done before the session is ever set up. That was one of Chet's fortes."

So it seems Chet wasn't just being modest in all those self-deprecating interviews like the one with Alanna Nash in her book *Behind Closed Doors*. "I knew a good song when I heard it," Atkins told Nash, "and I knew when to keep my mouth shut and let the artists and musicians come up with good arrangements, and occasionally I made a suggestion or two."

"I don't think Chet ever wanted to be a producer." said Sherrill. "He wanted to be a picker. He was a great guitar player and that was his first love. And I think he just produced out of necessity and because they needed him. I don't think he ever had the love of producing that Owen did or that I did. He wanted to play that guitar. I think he was right."

Owen Bradley was a role model for Sherrill, but Billy owed more to Bradley than just the production techniques he stole.

Bradley was directly responsible for Sherrill coming to Nashville in the early sixties.

"I was playing [sax] in a band in Hamilton, Alabama, making about thirty-five dollars a week. I had written this song, sent it to Tree [Publishing] called 'Your Sweet Love,'" recalled Sherrill. Billy didn't hear back, but Owen Bradley would put Sherrill's song on the B side of a hit single.

"So one day I got my mail in Hamilton, little mail box there, and there's a check in there from Tree Music for four thousand dollars. (chuckle) I said, 'I'm in the wrong town.'"

Once in Nashville, Sherrill got busy. With the help of a couple of friends he first set up a "demo studio" on top of a Masonic Lodge. He then sold the studio *to* and ran it *for* Sam Phillips—yeah, *that* Sam Phillips; produced *Classical Country*, his own album of classical instrumental takes on Buck Owens' hits (he'd wanted to call it *Bach Owens*)—went nowhere; and finally got hired by Epic as an in-house producer "for eight grand a year," inheriting a bunch of label bottom-feeders including a singer named David Houston.

"We weren't selling anything," recalled Sherrill.

Then Sherrill and Glen Sutton co-wrote "Almost Persuaded" for Houston. "We wrote it in one night, recorded it the next day, and it was out in three days," recalled Sherrill in a 1978 interview in *The Journal of Country Music*. The rest is your show biz history.

The song went to number one and stayed there for two months. Scholar Charles Wolfe described it as "the number one song of the year" (1966). It ended up winning Grammys for Best Country and Western Song, Best Country and Western Recording, and Best Country and Western Performance, Male.

As the sixties wound down, Sherrill produced six more number one singles for Houston and seven for his personal discovery Tammy Wynette. Then in the early seventies, Billy really hit a hot streak, producing seven number one singles for Charlie Rich in just two years (1973–74). By then Sherrill had more than arrived and he knew it.

Quonset Hut engineer Lou Bradley (no relation to Owen) tells a story about a *Rolling Stone* reporter who asked Billy what had changed in his life since he'd had all his success?

"The word 'love' has gone out of my vocabulary," Billy replied.

"What do you mean the word 'love' has gone out of your vocabulary?"

"I used to say I'd *love* to cruise the Greek islands, I'd *love* to go to Hawaii. Now I do it."

By the time George Jones joined the Epic label in the early seventies, Billy was as big, if not a bigger star businesswise, than George.

"I was about half scared of him. He was about half scared of me for a while. We didn't know each other," recalled Sherrill.

That fear soon gave way to elation in the wake of the standard Music City U.S.A. cure for all that ails you—all together now— "hit records."

14

MAKING MUSIC

During that first "He Stopped Loving Her Today" session at the Quonset Hut, Sherrill and the boys didn't take long to rough out the song. That's because there really wasn't much to it. Guitar player Pete Wade kept charts in a notebook for all of the thousands of songs he cut over the years. A normal song would "take like half a page," said Wade. Not "He Stopped Loving Her Today."

"There's a little bitty chart up in the corner. Sixteen bars," said Wade. "It's all the same thing over and over. The smallest one in the book, but yet the biggest song."

"It's not that complicated a song. Just a great song," said drummer Jerry Carrigan.

After Sherrill wrapped up the preliminary rundown in the studio, he said, "'Well, let me go into the control room and listen,'" recalled McCoy. "As he walked by, he stopped and he looked at me and he said, 'Get something on the second [half of the first] verse.' That was it. And so that's what I did."

Specifically, after George sang "He kept her picture on his wall," Charlie answered with a plaintive harmonica wail. This continued after each of the three remaining lines.

He kept her picture on his wall.
Went half crazy now and then.
He still loved her through it all,
Hoping she'd come back again.

Charlie wound up playing a three-note wail following the first, second, and fourth lines and a five-note wail following the third. Only fourteen notes in all.

(Now is that the only place you played?)

"Yeah," replied McCoy, "four very short, small little pieces. I think it's one of the best pieces of session work I've ever done."

This "call and response" kind of pattern was repeated throughout the song: the steel guitar, the Jordanaires, the violins, and even background singer Millie Kirkham reinforced (or in Millie's case, foreshadowed) the sentiment of each line Jones sang.

"I think you just let the music flow along with your story line and grow more intense as the lyric grows more intense. And then when you get reflective, like the recitation part, that's when you mellow back down," said Sherrill. "It's just something you try to weave into the song. Make the song more believable. . . . That's the only way I know how to do it."

As for this playing between the lines—literally—the technique was nothing new.

"That's pretty standard fare," said McCoy. "It's a fill: f-i-l-l, a fill. You know the secret to Nashville is that the fill guys play in between the words and not on top of 'em," said McCoy. "It's always been lyrics first."

"The song is the picture. Everything else is the frame," continued McCoy.

"The simplicity of production, and his [Sherrill's] arrangements: he doesn't clutter 'em up with an awful lot of fill instruments," said Kenny Rogers' producer Larry Butler in *How Nashville Became Music City U.S.A.* "He lets the tone of each instrument stand on its own, and whenever there is a fill, it says something."

Summing up, class, "You don't get in the way of a song," said McCoy. "When you come here and you wanta be a session player, if you don't learn that real quick, you're done before you begin."

• • •

Sherrill moved into the control room, where engineer Lou Bradley reigned over the hardware.

"It was a sixteen-bus, twenty-four inch console, and we had seven echo sends and returns," recalled Bradley.

[Say what?]

"I'd keep six E.M.T.'s and one live room, and I was probably one of the first guys there to quit printing reverb."

[Moving along.]

Once Sherrill got settled in, "We'd start off and we'd run it two or three times for them [engineers] to get their sound," said Bob Moore, "and then he'd say, 'Okay, let's cut one.' We'd cut one and then listen back to it. And alter. And cut another one and listen back to it and sometimes alter again."

"All I ever did was, instead of asking for 'input,'" said Sherrill, "[was] just say, 'Okay, do something,' and say, 'No, that's not right, do something else. Play it this way.' And they'll all do it."

"We were hired because every one of us had ideas," said Bob Moore. "[And] that's more or less where the producers came in was, uh, they would decide which idea was the best."

"He [Sherrill] had the nicest way of saying, 'I don't really like what you're doing, would you try something else,'" recalled drummer Jerry Carrigan. "He'd say, 'Carrigan, on that verse would you try it just for me, just try playing so-and-so instead of so-and-so and see what it sounds like.'"

Other days, it was "Carrigan, don't play that stuff like that. Save that for Miles Davis. I don't want all that fancy stuff. Don't play it. I don't wanta hear it."

There was no chance of Jerry Carrigan getting too fancy on "He Stopped Loving Her Today." While he had been playing drums for money since he was twelve, time was running out for the thirty-five-year-old Alabama native. It was his right arm. "All the nerves and everything was going bad," he said. Jerry had gone to the doctor looking for answers. What he got was questions.

"'Do you understand *worn out*?' [the doctor asked.] And I said, 'Yessir.' He said, 'That's what's wrong with it. It's worn out. You just played until it's *worn out.*' I said, 'Why did it happen to me?' He said, 'Well, why do some people have cancer? I can't answer that.' He said, 'It just happens to some people. Some people it doesn't happen to.'"

"I couldn't figure out any way I could play right-handed because my arm was hurting, so I turned around and played left handed," said Carrigan.

"I played a little march beat on the high hat [cymbal]," he recalled, "and then overdubbed the wood block. Then, of course, [played] regular drums on the chorus. The bass drum: I played it some in the verses."

"You don't just play whatever you want to on a song. That won't work," continued Carrigan. "You gotta play it—tailor it—for that situation, for the artist you're doing and for the way the song is. What this song is about."

And for "He Stopped Loving Her Today?"

"It's really a very sad song," said Carrigan. "That's why I played a drum part like a dirge."

"I thought, 'What kind of song was this?'" continued Carrigan. "It's a funeral song."

The very non-country woodblock comes in and is heard throughout the second verse (the lick coming on the fourth beat of every measure), goes away during the chorus, and then comes back on the spoken verse. Engineer Ron "Snake" Reynolds would claim credit for the woodblock, saying he played it with his finger during overdubs. (Not to worry, Reynolds was not only a union engineer, he was a member in good standing of the American Federation of Musicians Local 257.)

"I don't think he did, but I'm not gonna call him a liar," said Carrigan. "I've got the wood block in here in a box. I know that."

Maybe they're both right. The spoken verse would end up being recorded after the original tracking session and since Carrigan only played for one session for the song, Ron "Snake" Reynolds may have had to fill in on wood block.

For what it's worth.

As for George Jones, there was a problem that's been well-documented over the years. "Every time I'd try to get him to sing it," Sherrill told Jones biographer Bob Allen, "he'd end up singing [it to the melody of] the Kris Kristofferson classic, 'Help Me Make It Through the Night.'"

"This went on for a long time," said Sherrill. "He just couldn't seem to get it out of his head."

So, by Sherrill's account, that first go-around in the Quonset Hut would end up being a tracking session, where they recorded most everything but George's vocal for "He Stopped Loving Her Today."

"He was there when we put down the tracks. He came back in and redid his vocal," recalled guitarist Pete Wade.

(So he was probably never singing when the session musicians were playing [live].)

"Nah," said Sherrill.

(You'd laid all that down.)

"Yeah. He was in la-la land somewhere."

•   •   •

"It was the same crew whenever he could get them," said former Sherrill assistant Emily Mitchell of the hand-picked session musicians.

Emily would know. She had come to work for Sherrill in 1966 and, by the time "He Stopped Loving Her Today" was cut, she was "doing all the administrative work," since Billy didn't "wanta do anything but write songs and make music."

"That was where he was happiest," said Emily, "working in the studio and writing songs." So Emily would end up calling everybody, scheduling the studio, getting clearances for the songs, handling all the paperwork, and even dealing with the people in New York.

(You were doing Billy's job.)

(laugh) "Well, I didn't say that."

Why did Sherrill use the same session musicians all the time? "Well, they're the best," he said. "They were the most innovative, creative. And they went into sessions trying to make whoever sings, the singer, the artist, the star look good, not themselves." And heaven help the poor picker who dared, as Owen Bradley once put it, to "play anything fancy over any of my singers."

Like Bradley before him, Sherrill surrounded himself with musicians who knew him, the studio, and each other.

"The idea that the producers had: these guys are hand-picked. They know the studio. They know everything about how I operate in and out of the control room," said Bob Moore.

"You just felt at home," said piano player Pig Robbins of the Quonset Hut. "I guess because we worked so much there."

"We all fed off of each other. We were like brothers," said Moore of this group that had played together so often for so long that there was an almost psychic connection.

"I don't know of any time that Pig don't hear me before I hit a note," said Moore. "He knows exactly where I'm gonna go. Never, without fail, does he not go right with me and vice versa. If he does something, I just feel where he's gonna go."

Like Moore, Pig Robbins had been working with Sherrill from the beginning. Pig had played on Billy's first hit, David Houston's "Almost Persuaded," on Tammy's "D-I-V-O-R-C-E," on Charlie Rich's "Behind Closed Doors," and on dozens of other Sherrill-produced tunes. "If it wasn't for Pig Robbins, there wouldn't be no Billy Sherrill," said Bob Moore.

Even Pig disputes that—"Billy Sherrill's a helluva talent," he said—but you get the idea.

A native of Spring City, Tennessee, Robbins lost his sight at age three and started taking piano lessons at the Tennessee School for the Blind in Nashville when he was seven. He cut some rockabilly records as Mel "Pig" Robbins in the fifties, and a 1963 album, *A Bit of Country Piano*, before settling in as a session player.

"Pig is the best of the best," said Sherrill.

And no matter who the artist or what kind of music they were playing, Pig and the rest of Billy's lineup of session players was always pretty much the same.

(How was the instrumentation different on Charlie Rich and George Jones?)

"None, same guys," said Sherrill.

"You just learn to adapt to whatever song or artist that comes down the line," said Pig Robbins. "If you're gonna be successful in the studio [session player] business, you gotta be able to play some of all of it—gospel, country, pop, rock, whatever."

You have to be able to work with Perry Como in the morning and Johnny Paycheck in the afternoon. Session musicians are not rock, country, or R&B, they're musical mercenaries. There are no purists in studios.

And, yes, although Charlie Rich was a great piano player in his own right, Pig Robbins played keyboards on most of Rich's records. He felt the pressure. "With him standing about three feet behind me, the pucker factor was very high," said Robbins. Remember that opening lick on "Behind Closed Doors?" All Pig. The Country Music Hall of Fame's Recorded History Collection has a tape of the session and on it you can hear Pig and Billy going back and forth, editing, paring the opening down. Then Pig finally hits the famous lick and that moment of creation has the electricity of a first kiss.

Billy Sherrill's response to this magic moment, as preserved on tape for posterity: "Let's try it again without the giggles."

• • •

Born November 5, 1936, in Phil Campbell, Alabama, Billy Sherrill was one of four children. Billy's father traveled all over, spreading the gospel.

"He was like an evangelist," said Sherrill. "We'd go to Texas and he would preach, establish a church." And when his flock migrated north, Daddy would visit, "go like to Chicago and preach to all the people that knew him that went to Chicago to work," said Sherrill. "It wasn't like a continuous circuit type thing. But he did travel. We all traveled a lot."

Souls were saved.

"He'd do revivals. He had a tent," Sherrill continued. "Sometimes there'd be ten people there, twenty, sometimes five hundred," recalled Sherrill. "As it'd go, they'd go tell somebody and bring their friends back the next night.

"Had a sound system, kinda. Not much of one—a couple of amps. He didn't need much of one. He preached real loud."

Sherrill was a musical prodigy and his dad drafted him to play piano at services. It was just a matter of time before Billy's smartass DNA kicked in. And as Sherrill told journalist Michael Kosser, a young Billy once played "That's Where My Money Goes" when his dad was trying to take up the offering—"Got my butt whipped too,"—and "Bye Bye Blues" at a funeral. "There wasn't but about three people there and nobody recognized that one but my daddy," Sherrill said.

Sherrill was too soon on his own. "I was seventeen when my mother died. And twenty when my Daddy died," he said. Despite his religious heritage, when it came time to choose his music, sacred didn't stand a chance against profane. Why?

"Starvation. Do you realize what a Southern Baptist evangelist makes?" asked Sherrill, in an interview at mixonline.com. "I'm not talking Jim Bakker. My dad was being paid in cabbages and pigs, milk and fruit. There wasn't a whole lot of money in church music, but there was some in rock 'n' roll."

And apparently there was even more in square dancing, because that's how Billy was supporting himself—barely—when the four-thousand-dollar royalty check arrived from Tree and Billy picked up, moved to Nashville, and started making records and, well, you know, pissing people off—especially critics—with too-true-by-half quotes like this one from the May 1978 issue of the *Journal of Country Music*: "You don't go in and try to record what's great; you go in and try to record what's commercial, and to sell phonograph records. That's why they pay your salary. . . . You go in and try to figure out what people are looking for, what they want to buy. You try to put on the public's ears."

That's our Billy.

PART FIVE

GEORGE GLENN

15

PLUM CRAZY

During the same time Sherrill was trying to piece together "He Stopped Loving Her Today," he was also cutting a series of ten duets with George and partners Elvis Costello, Linda Ronstadt, James Taylor, Dr. Hook, Pop and Mavis Staples, Johnny Paycheck, Willie, Tammy, Waylon, and Emmylou for what would be *My Very Special Guests*. This album came at the end of a longstanding effort by CBS to take George and country music mainstream.

The idea was hatched in 1976 after CBS booked George at Willie Nelson's annual Fourth of July picnic to see how he would go over. This annual family reunion of the Outlaws pulled in eighty thousand pot-smoking, long-haired country boys (and girls) and a lot of national press. While not thought to be a George Jones kind of crowd, he was a huge hit and, before the end of the year, Jones would become the darling of the mainstream media.

Suddenly George Jones was everywhere. "He is the spirit of country music, plain and simple, its true Holy Ghost," said *Penthouse*. He "should be on a list of America's all-time, top ten best singers" in any category, said the *Village Voice*. "The best country singer in the world," said *People*.

"We live in the midst of so much bullshit, and then there's George," CBS publicist Sue Binford told Jones biographer Dolly Carlisle. "This guy was stripped down and down to earth and made no bones about it."

Capitalizing on the buzz, CBS cranked it up a notch, and in 1977 George became the first country artist ever booked at the Bottom Line in New York, then the premiere folk music showcase in the U.S. Everybody who was anybody in the media and music biz was invited to the shows on September 6–7, 1977, including *Time, Newsweek*, and the *New York Times*, and luminaries like

Linda Ronstadt, Elton John, James Taylor, Emmylou Harris, the entire cast from *Saturday Night Live,* and newscasters Walter Cronkite and John Chancellor.

George didn't show up.

"Of all the people I've ever recorded in my life," Billy Sherrill told Dolly Carlisle, "I think George Jones cares the least about ambition."

Executives at CBS in New York were worried that George had his shot and blew it. His career was over. Wrong. "No Show Jones" became a media hero for standing up the New York elite. The duets album was supposed to keep that ball a-rollin'. Didn't happen.

"He was wrecked the whole album," recalled Sherrill. Couldn't sing a lick. (Well, relatively speaking. He was still George Jones, after all.)

Anyway, "Couldn't sing?" Didn't matter.

The president of CBS called Billy. "'We have got to have an album on George Jones,' he said. I said, 'All I've got is this duets album. I want to get him in when he's feeling better and re-sing his parts 'cause he's hoarse, he's messed up.'"

"'We've got to have it. I don't care how bad it is, we gotta have product.'"

"And against my better judgment, we put the damn thing out. I didn't like it at all," said Sherrill.

The album hit the shelves on December 1, 1979. Around this same time, George also cut some of the tunes that would show up on the *I Am What I Am* album in 1980. Sherrill produced all this while George was having trouble singing, especially on "He Stopped Loving Her Today."

That wasn't like the old George.

"Most of his vocals, he didn't have trouble with," said engineer Snake Reynolds. "And he'd get 'em on while we were cutting the [instrumental] tracks."

But there would be nothing usual about the making of "He Stopped Loving Her Today." After trying to sing it to the tune of "Help Me Make It Through the Night," George finally learned the melody. Then they had to catch him on a day when he could actually sing.

"That was during George's rocking time. So there was no predicting what shape he'd be in when he came in," said Reynolds.

"It [cocaine] ruined his voice. For years, it ruined his voice," said Sherrill. "It happened to a lot of them. It happened to Paycheck. I'm not gonna name a bunch of names, because some of them are dead. . . . They come in and they [whispers hoarsely] sound like that."

Sherrill had some very unfatherly advice for his stable of singers.

"Get on the heavy stuff. Your heroin. Shoot up instead of puttin' that damn powder in your throat. That's what ruins your voice. 'Well, I may try that.' I'm not trying to tell you to get off drugs. Just get on something and quit ruining your voice."

But George was way too far gone to listen to Daddy-Billy. He had moved on. Now he was seeking counsel from an alter ego he called Deedoodle the Duck.

"He talked like a duck many times in my office," said Sherrill.

"If he wanted me to do something that he didn't wanta tell me," continued Sherrill, "he'd have the duck tell me."

(Like a ventriloquist's dummy?)

"Yeah. That type thing. Alter ego type thing."

George's manager at the time, Alcy Benjamin "Shug" (as in sugar) Baggott, got his own dose of duck. "Every now and then, he would say something nasty to me as Donald Duck and then apologize as George Jones," Baggott told Jones biographer Dolly Carlisle. "He would look at me and say, 'Shug, I told him not to talk to you like that.'"

George showcased Deedoodle the Duck at an April 6, 1979, "comeback appearance" at the Exit In in Nashville.

"Well, first of all, they like to never got him out there," recalled Pig Robbins, chuckling. "And when he did come out, he sang everything in the duck—Donald Duck voice."

Seems the duck could remember the lyrics when George couldn't. That stunt got him "carried away in a straight jacket," Baggott told Carlisle. Then in June, George and the Duck and Waylon Jennings showed up on Ralph Emery's syndicated radio show, as reported by Bob Allen in his Jones biography.

EMERY: "Did you bring 'the Duck' with you today?"

GEORGE: "Yeah! Oh, yeah! I just couldn't leave home without him. 'The Old Man' too. They just stay with me all the time."

EMERY: "Deedoodle?"

GEORGE: "Yeah. He's first cousins to Donald."

EMERY: "Does he sing?"

WAYLON: "Yeah, he sings. Make him sing, George."

GEORGE: (in the Donald Duck squawk): "I love you so much, it hurts me."

"The Old Man" was a second alter ego George had conjured up. With the addition of the Old Man, things had gotten even more strange. Now you might find the Old Man arguing with Deedoodle the Duck while George refereed.

"They had personalities and passionate convictions of their own," said George in his autobiography. "Neither would take shit off of the other."

"He sat alone in his car for hours as he, 'the Duck' and 'The Old Man' debated furiously among themselves," wrote biographer Bob Allen.

Plum crazy.

George Jones was losing his voice? Couldn't sing? That was the least of his problems. After decades of following in the footsteps of his idol Hank Williams, it had all finally caught up with him. How did this happen? How did the greatest country singer of all time end up in this sorry state? It had taken every one of his forty-eight years.

16

SPOILED ROTTEN CHILD PRODIGY ADDICT

> The more anguish I underwent in my
> personal life, the more my career flourished.
> —GEORGE JONES

George Glenn Jones, the second son and youngest of eight, was born on September 12, 1931, in Saratoga, Texas, to George Washington and Clara Patterson Jones. He weighed in at twelve pounds, and maybe that had something to do with the doctor dropping him and breaking his arm. It would not be George Glenn's last fall.

He was born into a mixed marriage: his mama a born-again Christian, his daddy a hopeless alcoholic who had developed a drinking problem after his favorite child, first-born daughter Ethel, died of malaria five years before George Glenn came along.

"From the day he was born, George Glenn Jones was a mama's boy," wrote Jones biographer Dolly Carlisle. "Spoiled," said family friend Katy Hooks. "Overprotected," said sister Helen who, along with her four younger sisters, two sets of twins (Joyce and Loyce and Doris and Ruth), likely had a lot to do with spoiling and over-protecting the baby of the family.

There was music from the beginning. Daddy, George Washington, played guitar and harmonica; and mama, Clara Patterson, sang and played piano and organ at the White Oak Baptist Church.

"All those Pattersons could sing," Katy Hooks told Carlisle.

And they were serious about it.

"If I had a kid that couldn't sing, I would have to get rid of him," one of Clara's brothers said.

Not to worry.

"Glenn could carry a tune by the time he was a year old,"
recalled Hooks. "Clara teached George a song called 'Billy Boy'
and he was singing that song when he was a year."

George Glenn's musical education continued at church. "I
loved those churches when I was a kid, because they loved to
sing," George told Sirius DJ Charlie Monk. "I did what they called
back then, they called 'em 'specials.' 'George, you're gonna do a
special for us Sunday.'"

It was a good thing George Glenn had an aptitude for music,
because traditional education was never his thing.

"My first year in school earned me a report card with an F in
every single subject and an F in conduct, which was as bad as you
could get, but, you see, we didn't care for learning," George told
the *Music City News* in 1966.

When George Glenn was seven, the family got its first radio,
"a big, crude-looking, battery operated machine," wrote Jones
biographer Bob Allen. A Zenith, said George. You could now
add the Grand Ole Opry to the musical influences of family and
church.

"I'd crawl in bed between Mama and Daddy and we'd hear
the Opry on that old radio we had," said George. "I'd tell Mama,
'If I fall asleep before Roy Acuff or Bill Monroe comes on, be sure
and wake me up!'"

In 1941, the family moved to Kountze, Texas, where the
masthead of the local newspaper proudly declared: "We're not
the gateway to anything." But the town would prove to be a gateway for George Glenn. The ten-year-old hooked up with Brother
Byrle and Sister Annie Stephens, the couple behind the Kountze
Full Gospel Tabernacle, and soon began his first regularly scheduled public performances, first singing in church and then on
street corners.

"People sometimes blocked the sidewalks to hear him," Sister
Annie told Allen.

The Jones family followed the work to big city Beaumont,
population around eighty thousand, where George Glenn got his
first guitar on his eleventh birthday: a "three-quarter size Gene

Autry guitar," reported Allen, a gift from his father. He would earn it.

George Glenn learned his first few chords during a return visit to Sister Annie's and "a few weeks later she was amazed to see that he could already play the small instrument better than she could," wrote Allen.

A prodigy.

Once he had a guitar, George became as hooked on music as he would on cocaine thirty-some years later. "What had been an infatuation was now an obsession," wrote Dolly Carlisle.

An addict.

"I didn't want to do anything else," George told Carlisle. "You could have whupped me, beat me to death. Nothing was going to make me quit loving that guitar. That's all I wanted to do."

"He was different from other kids. He didn't get out and run and play like most kids," said sister Helen.

"I just wanted to go out in the woods and hide and play the guitar," recalled George. "That was more important to me than anything in the world."

George would soon be singing for tips on the streets and city buses of Beaumont. Then there were the advanced studies with his father, maestro George Washington Jones, who would bully George Glenn and, at times, the other kids into singing for him.

"When he come in drunk, he'd say, 'Get up and sing me some songs,'" George Glenn said of his father. George Glenn hated it, but years later his older brother, Herman, insisted these late night concerts-on-demand "helped George a lot, 'cause he played more and got more practice."

The arrival of the guitar soon would mean the end of George Glenn's formal schooling. "I just couldn't think of nothing but that guitar and music," George told Carlisle. After George flunked out of the seventh grade, his mother Clara "let him quit" school. No job stuck.

"For about three years there after he got out of school he was just singing at one place or another," sister Helen told Dolly Carlisle. "Anything he could do concerning music, he'd love it. He'd go do it. Otherwise he didn't do anything."

"It's been music all the way. I've never done anything but pick and sing," George told the *Music City News* in 1966.

The year he turned sixteen, George Glenn would reach his full size of five feet seven, 140 pounds; play his first radio gig; sing in his first honky tonk; and, according to friend and fellow musician Dalton Henderson, drink his first beer.

"Sometimes, George would have a few drinks in one of those beer joints and it would change his personality so much that it scared me," Henderson told Jones biographer Bob Allen. "All it took was for somebody to say something he didn't like and he'd be ready to fight."

That same year, George Glenn would turn pro. In those days, there were two places where George's variety of singing was in demand: churches and honky tonks. One paid a little better.

"I was really wantin' to sing gospel music and things just didn't go that way," George told Sirius DJ Charlie Monk.

Instead, for seventeen dollars and change a week, George took a job playing lead guitar for Eddie and Pearl, a husband and wife radio duo that also performed at local honky tonks.

"She played the big bull bass. He played guitar with his harp [harmonica] in the rack," recalled George.

By the late forties George was out on his own, a struggling honky tonk singer. "Back then, he was just a happy-go-lucky cat who was just in it for the music, the beer, and the broads, just like the rest of us," musician Huey Meaux told Bob Allen.

George met Dorothy Bonvillian while performing at Playground Park in Beaumont. The two married in June 1950, separated in May 1951, and welcomed baby Susan in October of that same year. George was twenty years old. The divorce papers would describe him as "a man of violent temper . . . addicted to the drinking of alcoholic beverages." After being jailed twice for not paying wife Dorothy's court-ordered upkeep, George was forced to join the Marines in November 1951.

When the Marines screwed up and sent all of his paycheck—fifteen dollars every two weeks—back home to ex-wife Dorothy, George Glenn improvised, going AWOL to sing in San Jose, California, to "pick up twenty-five dollars a night whenever I could appear. It was the only thing I had to live on."

George was honorably discharged in 1953 and, back home in Beaumont, he signed with Pappy Daily, the "Day" part of the Starday label. They would be together for nineteen years.

"I've had lots of people say that I made George Jones," said Pappy. "I says, 'No, I didn't make him. I just gave him a chance.'"

George soon began making recordings in what Bob Allen described as a "crude back-porch studio" at the home of Jack Starnes, the "Star" part of Starday. He made an impression on George Baxter, a figure in the local music scene.

"He wore a flattop, and his eyes were so big and so close together that they kind of looked like you were looking into a big double-barreled shotgun," Baxter told Allen. "Only when you did look into them, you kinda got the impression there was not much going on in there. But then he came up to the microphone and went up on his tiptoes and began to sing and I was just amazed! I could hear a clarity and beauty in his voice that just gave me chill bumps."

In the fall of 1954, "after a two-week courtship," wrote Allen, George took a second wife, marrying Shirley Corley, an eighteen-year-old carhop he met at Princess Drive-in in Houston. The marriage didn't work out, but it would drag on for fourteen years, yielding two kids: Jeffrey (1955) and Bryan (1958).

After George wrote and cut his first hit song, "Why Baby Why?" in 1955, he was booked as a regular on the Louisiana Hayride in Shreveport, appearing with the likes of Elvis and Johnny Cash. The next year he became a regular on the Grand Ole Opry. He was on his way in more ways than one as he sang, drank, and fought his way across the country music landscape.

"Back in those days with George, you couldn't tell what that little bastard was liable to do," recalled Gabe Tucker, a promoter for Starday.

George had his first number one record, "White Lightning," in 1959. He remembered sixty-four takes. Biographer Tom Carter said it took eighty three. Whatever. Everybody agrees there were so many that bass player and future Tree publishing executive Buddy Killen blistered his fingers hitting the opening lick. What was the problem? "George was drunk during the recording session," wrote Carter.

George scored his second number one record, "Tender Years," in 1961, and, in 1962, his third number one song, "She Thinks I Still Care," was named the year's Favorite Country Music Single and earned George recognition as the year's Favorite Male Country Artist in *Billboard*'s annual awards poll.

George Jones had arrived. He was now a bona fide country music star with his own band, his own bus, and his own country-music-size drinking problem. Well, "problem" may not be the right word. Ask around. For George Jones, drinking was not always a problem. At times it was a gift. An asset. The keys to the kingdom.

. . .

The day after man discovered fire he lit up the first funny cigarette, and ever since then we've been hearing tales of folks using various foreign substances in hopes of revving up the creative process. Sometimes it works.

When asked it he ever thought about giving up drugs, gonzo journalist Hunter S. Thompson glanced over at the satchel holding his drug stash and told an interviewer, "Without that I'd have the brain of a second-rate accountant."

LSD was described as "a shortcut to enlightenment" by *One Flew Over the Cuckoo's Nest* novelist Ken Kesey. "There's something about seeing reality with a new light shined on it," he said.

One more from just down the street.

"They were giants," said session musician Charlie McCoy of *Blonde on Blonde*, *John Wesley Harding*, and *Nashville Skyline*, the three albums Bob Dylan cut in Nashville in the sixties. McCoy played on all three, and a few years back he ended up at this Bob Dylan colloquium in Europe.

"A British guy, he says, 'We can prove that Bob Dylan's writings go back to Homer, the Greek, the Greek people.' And I'm sitting there saying, 'This is the biggest bunch of crap I've ever heard in my life.'

"I said, 'Hey, you guys left out one thing, one common thread through Bob's career. And they were like, 'Oh, what! What! What!' and I said, 'Drugs.'"

Which brings us back to George Jones. From all reports, back in the olden days, George sang better in the studio after he'd had a couple.

"Yeah. It'd loosen him up," said session drummer Jerry Carrigan.

"I remember back in the Pappy Daily years, he'd get about two sheets to the wind. Man, he could moan his ass off," said session pianist Pig Robbins.

"Jones is a very, extremely shy person," said Billy Sherrill. "And uh, I'm sure after a couple of shots of vodka or somethin', there's a certain time there before he has too much that he's really laid back and puts feeling—more feeling in a song. I think a lot of people are like that."

Although I figured George would deny it—doesn't want to set a bad example for America's youth and all that—I put the question to him directly.

(Pig and Billy say you sang a little better after you'd had a couple of drinks.)

"That was true. I was awful shy when I first came to Nashville."

(Did it help you out in the studio?)

"Yes, it did," he replied. "But I would only have two or three small ones to relax me. And, of course, a lot of times it'd get to where you overdo it sometimes."

Exhibit A.

"It was getting to be one o'clock in the morning and George was getting drunker and drunker," recalled stand-up bass player Bob Moore.

They were hours into the session and, forget finishing the first song, "He couldn't even get through the first verse he was so drunk," said Moore.

Finally, Bob parked his bass, marched into the control room, and confronted producer Pappy Daily. Broad shouldered, about six two, Bob might have been intimidating if he and Pappy hadn't been drinking buddies.

"I said, 'Well, what would you think if I took my bass and went home?'" recalled Moore. "He said, 'I'd applaud you.'"

Still they decided to give George one last chance.

"Well, we got about four bars into it," continued Moore, "and he screwed it up. And he said. 'Okay, let's do it again.' I said, 'Good night,' and I walked out."

Hell was raised.

"The union called me. 'Whataya mean walking out on a session?'" But it soon blew over. "George came in the next day and apologized to everybody," continued Moore, "and everything was all right."

Until the next time.

"George would just get so drunk he didn't know where he was or who he was. And he didn't care. Of course, no drunk does," said Moore.

"I've seen him that way [drunk] on several occasions. I remember on a song he did, 'Walk Through This World With Me' [1967] (laugh)," said Pig Robbins, "I don't know how many times we cut that."

"Sometimes they'd just send him home, y'know. He'd just be too out of it," recalled drummer Jerry Carrigan.

"I never saw George take a drink or a drug," said Carrigan. "I never *saw* him do it. I just saw the aftermath of it."

It would be decades before George Jones got sober. He wasn't alone. In the fall of 1984, the *Tennessean* did a series of stories on what it called "Music City's High Life." Since 1978, said the newspaper, "illicit drugs—chiefly marijuana and cocaine—have flooded the [music] industry." Some were in it for the fun, others were in it for the money, while still others meant to jump-start their "second rate accountant brains" in hopes of producing, if not art, at least charted records.

17

HEART BROKE

Been down so long it looks like up to me.

—RICHARD FARINA, novelist

George and Tammy married, each for the third time, on February 16, 1969.

"I was in love with her before I ever met her," George told biographer Dolly Carlisle. "I loved her singing."

"Tammy loved George Jones, the singer," Joan Dew, the co-author of Tammy's autobiography, *Stand By Your Man*, told Carlisle. "She idolized him. He was the epitome of the great country singer. What would anyone do if they had a chance to have an affair with their idol? I'm real doubtful about whether she loved George Jones, the man."

Daughter Georgette was born in 1970, and in late 1971 George signed with Tammy's label (Epic) so the two could record together. As part of the bargain, George got a cocky, talented, producer/label chief, and soon-to-become lifelong-friend Billy Sherrill. By the end of the year Epic would release "Take Me," the first of eleven charted duets George and Tammy would record in the next seven years.

Despite his love for Tammy, George hung on to the other woman: Clara Patterson Jones. "Mama was the only one who could settle me down," wrote George in his autobiography. "She'd hold my hand, call me Glenn (she always called me by my middle name), and tell me that she and Jesus loved me. I might have been filled with rage, but the sight of her presence and the sound of her voice never failed to soothe me. Like a child, I would often fall asleep."

"George never loved another woman like he loved his mama," George's aunt, Josie Marcontell, told Jones biographer Bob Allen. "She was his strength. When she was alive, she talked to him and straightened him out when nobody else could. But after she was gone, he just went to pieces. He didn't have nobody to love him."

George's mother died in April 1974. "Nothing was ever the same," Tammy told Carlisle.

Heart broke.

A year later, George's marriage to Tammy was over. Post divorce, George "was like a schoolboy in love with some girl that didn't want him," said Tammy's lawyer, John Lentz. "Nobody had ever done that to him before."

Heart broke times two.

•   •   •

In the spring of 1975 George hooked up with Shug Baggott, a club manager, who got George to lend his name to a new club called Possum Holler on Printer's Alley in Nashville. In time, Shug would become first George's manager, and then his drug dealer, introducing George to cocaine in 1977, according to George's autobiography. In the short term, that was good for business because George could be "staggering drunk," snort a little coke, and still get out on stage and perform.

"Felt like I could go twelve rounds with Muhammad Ali," said George.

Shug would develop a cocaine habit of his own. "It was fun. It was a lot of fun," he told Carlisle. But the drugs were not only fun, they were a business opportunity, and Shug soon started dealing to clients who, shall we say, demanded a certain amount of discretion. Shug's last client turned out to be an FBI agent. Dolly Carlisle turned up an affidavit claiming Baggott sold two pounds of coke to the agent for $58,000. Baggott would end up doing time in federal prison after pleading guilty to possession of cocaine with intent to distribute. It was all over the papers.

Meanwhile, George kept trying to win Tammy back. In May 1976, he bought her a gold Thunderbird he couldn't afford for her thirty-fourth birthday. In November of that same year, even after

Tammy had married and divorced Michael Tomlin, who Carlisle described as "a handsome, young, Nashville real estate broker," George dropped everything and flew to England to be by her side when she took sick on an European tour.

"There will never be anyone else for either of us," George told British reporters. "No one for her. No one for me."

Pitiful.

George was still hung up on Tammy in 1977. "I may as well admit it," he told Joan Dew in an interview in the August issue of *Country Music*. "I still love her and that ain't gonna change, no matter what happens in her personal life or mine."

Then in 1978, as rumors of "an impending George-and-Tammy reunion continued to swirl feverishly," as Bob Allen phrased it, Ms. Wynette married her fifth and final husband, George Richey, a Music Row insider "who had written many of [George] and Tammy's biggest hits." Prior to her marriage to Richey, George and Tammy had maintained a friendship. That wouldn't last. Here's George's side.

"He [Richey] told me on the phone, 'We don't want you calling here no more and we don't want you around here no more,'" recalled George in a 1979 interview with Bob Allen.

Later in that same phone call, according to George, Richey told George to stay away from Tammy and George's daughter Georgette.

"I said, 'I'll die and go to hell,'" recalled George.

In time, after it became clear Tammy's marriage to Richey would stick, that George and Tammy were never going to get back together, George lost it.

"I just didn't care anymore," said George in *Same Ole Me*, the authorized video biography.

The man who for twenty years had made a living singing about other people's broken hearts now had one of his very own. He was almost ready to sing "He Stopped Loving Her Today."

• • •

The piling on began in August 1978. A month after Tammy married Richey, she sued George for nonpayment of $36,000 in child support. Then local furniture dealer John F. Lawhon sued him for $13,554.35. The IRS soon joined the fun. George claimed his manager, Shug Baggott, was supposed to be paying everybody. (This was a year before Baggott's cocaine bust.) Shug said there was nothing to pay them with.

"Right at this point, George Jones doesn't have any assets except his voice," Baggott told the *Nashville Banner*.

And George not only wasn't cashing in on that asset: his voice, in a backhanded way, was actually costing him money. In January 1979, the *Tennessean* reported that George, the man some were now calling No Show Jones, had rolled up thousands in debt as promoters sued him "for missing some sixty-nine show dates in the last two years, fifty of them in 1977." Long story short, bankruptcy was on the horizon even before the Holiday Inn in Muddy, Illinois, sued George for $37.50.

Yawn. How about some gunplay?

• • •

It may come from a friend or relative in the first throes of con-version—absolutely giddy, or from a saucer-eyed evangelical who knocked on your door two minutes before. But if you've spent any time in the South, where proselytizing is part and parcel of religion, chances are somebody at some time or other has tried to convince you to "accept Jesus as 'Your Own Personal Savior.'" "You too, can be saved!" they say. "Born again!" All that. If you've ever heard such a pitch, then you understand why somebody—anybody—after being confronted over and over and over and over and over by a friend or relative or saucer-eyed evangelical who just won't give it a rest, might, say, in a weak, perhaps drunken moment, raise up a righteous sidearm and take a potshot at said friend or relative or saucer-eyed evangelical.

Thursday, September 14, 1978, the banks of Cypress Creek near Florence, Alabama. It was after midnight on a sweltering fall night when the two men faced each other from the driver's seat of their respective cars: the drug-addled George Jones in his tan Lincoln Town Car; the born-again Peanutt Montgomery in his silver Pontiac Trans Am. The two men had a long history.

Peanutt was the brother of George's sixties duet partner Melba Montgomery and the brother-in-law of George's then girlfriend, Linda Welborn. For years Peanutt had been George's best friend, co-songwriter, and drinking buddy. But not lately. Now George called the suddenly pious Peanutt "Little Jesus," tired of Montgomery treating him like just another soul in need of saving.

In George's version of the story, Peanutt shouted, "You need Jesus! Repent! Repent! Repent!" Then, both agree, George shouted, "See if your God can save you now!" just before he took a shot at Peanutt with a .38 caliber Smith and Wesson at point blank range.

There's a photograph on page 35 of the January–February 1979 issue of *Country Music* magazine showing Peanutt looking out the driver's side window of his silver Trans Am. He looks to be sitting exactly the way he was the night the shot was fired. The bullet hole, just below the window frame, is dead center of Peanutt's chest.

"Had the path of the bullet been two inches up or down, Montgomery would probably be dead today," reported Bill Jarnigan.

Looking at that picture, you can't help thinking George Jones is one very lucky man. Anybody else would have been getting out on parole just about now after doing thirty years hard time for murdering their best friend. Peanutt filed, but then dropped, charges of assault with intent to murder. George walked. As it should be, he said.

"I believe with all of my heart that someone, possibly someone in law enforcement, doctored that picture to try to help me get my thinking right," wrote George in his autobiography.

How 'bout them Vols?

•   •   •

"I know I've disappointed a lot of people, but I hope my fans will judge me for what I do next year—1979—not what I've done for the past four years," Jones told the *Nashville Banner* in late 1978. George might have been better off delaying that judgment. "George's horror story continued through 1979," as biographer

Dolly Carlisle put it, getting more horrific by the minute. "By mid 1979, Nashville was flooded with speculation that George wouldn't live out the year," wrote Carlisle. The reasons: "too much alcohol" and "too much cocaine," both meant to soothe a broken heart. And before the year ended, most agreed, 1979 would be the worst year of George's life.

"That was during George's wild times. He would show up every once and a while from the road and try to sing and sometimes we'd get a few lines here and there," recalled engineer Ron "Snake" Reynolds. "[And] sometimes we wouldn't get anything."

Working with George had always required patience. He was no picnic to manage even when he was sober. To hear Billy Sherrill tell it, Sherrill had spent better than twenty years trying to coax George Jones into the studio.

(How did you schedule him?)

"We didn't. We scheduled a session and most of the time, he wouldn't even be there. But then we'd do the tracks [musical accompaniment] anyway," said Sherrill.

"It takes forever for him to get in the mood to do it," continued Sherrill.

(He had to be in the mood?)

"Yeah, I'd say so."

(Well, that doesn't sound like a pro.)

"Well, I don't think 'pro' is what he was."

This in a town full of pros, musicians who pride themselves on being able to play and sing whatever, whenever. Not George Jones.

"He hated to be pinned down," continued Sherrill. "[You can't say], 'you've got to be here Thursday at two o'clock.' And I always hated that too. Just give him enough rope and he'll finally come around on his own time. He calls me. 'Well, I been singing this thing in the car. I know it. Get some studio time and I'll go in and do it.' This happened on many, many occasions."

"Once it's his idea, he'll show," Sherrill told Michael Kosser.

"You couldn't say, 'Okay, we've got to do this,'" Billy said. "Then, he'd just space out and not do anything. You'd have to say, [real low]. 'We need to do this some of these days, when we get around to it.'

[Dumb George voice] "'Well, uh, what about now?'

"'Okay, if you want to.'"

A quick clarification. While some of the things Billy Sherrill says about George Jones might look a little harsh in print, they don't come off that way in person. Sherrill loves the man (you can hear it in his tone of voice, see it in his demeanor) and the two still hang out together. Despite that, Sherrill is forever telling stories in which he casts himself as the learned sage fast approaching the end of his patience and George as his not-so-bright acolyte.

"One time Jones came out of the studio after doing a real, real good reading on a couple of songs and he was—had his chest stuck out and he was happy. He said [Dumb George voice], 'That was good, man. I think, that's gonna be good—blah, blah, blah.' I said [learned sage voice], 'Jones, with all the success you've had lately, not having to work too hard for it,' I said, 'Do you ever think you oughta be grateful and thank God for your success, for what's happened to you?' He said, 'You know, you're right. One of these days I'm gonna get around to doing that.'"

"I've got a record, an old record of his on Starday. And he hates it," said Sherrill, singing a few bars. "He sounds so whiny he made Bill Monroe sound like Ernest Tubb. Anyway, when we get to arguing I say, 'Jones here's what you sounded like before we met.' 'Well you gimme that damn tape.' 'I got other copies. It don't matter.' It'd make him so mad when I played that. Yeah, I made him sing lower and lower and lower," said Sherrill.

"When he got to feeling good, he'd come in and say, 'Okay, let's go in [the studio],' and he wouldn't know it [the song]," said Sherrill.

'Kinda hard to overdub a song, Jones, if you haven't learned it.'

'Well, you know I played it a couple of times.'

"He wasn't a very fast study like Tammy, some of the others. You play her a song once and she could sing it back to you," said Sherrill.

Once Sherrill, a reformed rock 'n' roll sax player himself, overdubbed a sax on a Jones record. Jones went nuts.

"When he heard it, he wanted to kill me. He said, 'You ruined me. All the little old ladies who buy my records, they hate the saxophone.' I said, 'No, they don't.' He argued and carried on and stomped and raised hell (had a few drinks by then). [Dumb George voice] 'Well, leave the damn thing on there.' I said, 'I intend to.'"

While George was under contract to CBS, that didn't mean much. Counting releases during that era, it looks like the label was shooting for two albums, a total of about twenty songs, a year. But "It was not much of a contract," recalled Sherrill. "I think it just required whatever we could get together and do. They knew Jones, his personality. They knew they might get one album or none or three. So they just left it up to me."

"They knew what was going on. They knew the story. They knew I'd get him in when I could. They knew I'd do the best dang stuff I could do on him and they left me alone. I spent twenty, twenty-five years with a record company and never felt like I had a boss."

Did Sherrill ever have trouble communicating with the big boys in New York? "Nah, we just didn't talk. If they didn't like what I did, it went out anyway," said Sherrill. "They weren't gonna fire me, because they were making money. So they just left me alone. I never had budget problems. I never sent in budgets. I just spent what I needed to spend, which was a fraction of what the producer in New York would spend on the same thing."

And sometimes there were real bargains to be had. Like in 1975.

"I picked up Willie Nelson's *Red Headed Stranger* album for seventeen thousand dollars," said Sherrill. "He produced it and we picked it up to distribute."

Billy didn't think much of the album, but he sent it to New York anyway. The CBS guy called back and said, "'That's the worst thing I've ever heard,'" recalled Sherrill. "I said [chuckle], 'Yeah, you're right.'"

Willie had cut the album down in Garland, Texas, using his road band, which was not exactly studio friendly, and a loose production style that was the polar opposite of Billy's approach. Sherrill believed in a place for every note and every note in its place. Willie didn't.

"Willie Nelson is the country equivalent of the Rolling Stones," said songwriter Bobby Braddock. "The Beatles were very tight. The Stones were very loose. It was all great music. It was just a different thing. . . . It's not disciplined music."

In Sherrill's telling, he talked New York into biting the bullet on *Red Headed Stranger* just to keep Willie happy. "I said, 'Y'know, it's big out in Texas, maybe we can get our money back just in the Southwest.'[The CBS guy said] 'Yeah, just put it out. Don't say much about it. Maybe it'll go away.' Damn thing went gold, platinum," as in sold a million-some records.

In his autobiography, Willie tells a little different story. He has Sherrill and the label arguing against releasing the album saying, "it was under produced, too sparse." (That's label-speak for "the worst thing I ever heard.") But Willie refused to budge since his contract gave him artistic control.

Turned out Willie was beyond right. Not only did the album sell, a generation later somebody over at CMT named *Red-Headed Stranger* the number one country album of all time. So other than sales and critical acclaim, Sherrill had it about right.

Fellow "Outlaw" Waylon Jennings came from the same keep-it-loose school as Willie. [Hyperbole alert.] "He once took a gun to a recording session and threatened to blow the fingers off Music Row's A-Team players," reported one historian. "Jennings wanted the artistic freedom to record his own songs with his own band in his own style. He was inspired to pursue this after visiting Willie Nelson in Texas."

But performers' loyalty to their road bands is not just about art. It's also about keeping the paychecks coming when the band's not on tour.

"They wanted to keep their guys workin'," said session bass player Bob Moore. "It's about money."

The irony of all this is that *Red Headed Stranger*, the breakthrough album for Mr. Outlaw, as portrayed by Willie Nelson, was being distributed by a beyond-establishment label, CBS, with the help of Mr. Music Row, Billy Sherrill. What kind of outlaw rebellion was that? Somebody called it a rebellion of sons against fathers. Let's call it a paper rebellion led by the platoon of "marketeers" who came up with the term "Outlaw" and then bombarded the media with thousands of press releases and a bunch of great records. The music *was* different, no arguing that, but the people making and selling it? Nashville's finest. (Willie Nelson an "outlaw"? The man wrote "Crazy," the Nashville Sound anthem, for God's sake.)

PART SIX

THE MAKING OF
"HE STOPPED
LOVING
HER TODAY"

18

NOW IN SESSION: GEORGE JONES

I could hear the whole record in my head before we got to
the studio. Getting it out of my head was sometimes kind of hard.
—BILLY SHERRILL to the *Tennessean*'s Peter Cooper in 2008.

In late 1979, George Jones stopped showing up at all. "He was
subsisting off a diet of crackers, roasted peanuts, and canned sar-
dines for weeks at a time," wrote biographer Bob Allen. "He had
walking pneumonia, his gums would sometimes bleed from mal-
nutrition, his weight had dropped from 145 pounds all the way
down to ninety eight."

At times homeless and destitute, living out of his car, George
continued waving a handgun around, threatening to kill himself
and others. Witnesses spotted him loitering on Music Row, chatting it up with an eight-by-ten glossy of Hank Williams.

Finally, mercifully, on December 11, 1979, in a move that
probably saved George's life, Peanutt Montgomery summoned
the men in white coats.

"Do you love this man?" the judge had asked Peanutt at the
commitment hearing, according to George's autobiography.

"Yes, I love him," Peanutt replied.

George was declared a ward of the state and was placed in
the Eliza Coffee Memorial Hospital in his hometown of Florence,
Alabama. Four days later he was transferred to Hill Crest, "an
exclusive three-hundred-dollar-a-day private psychiatric hospital" in Birmingham. (Friends would foot the bill.) The diagnosis, reported Carlisle: ". . . an acute paranoid state with suicidal
and homicidal potential to a high degree. He was suffering from
delirium tremens, secondary to chronic and acute heavy intake of

alcohol, and his admitting diagnosis also included the suspicion of chronic use of cocaine."

George stayed through Christmas. He stayed through New Year's. "'This is it,' I remember thinking near the end of my hospitalization, 'I have finally reached the bottom,'" George wrote in his autobiography. On January 2, 1980, three weeks into what doctors thought might be a six-week stay, George was set free.

"I have seen the light," said George.

Yeah, and the light was neon and read COLD BEER. George bought a six-pack on the way home and soon picked up where he left off with his cocaine habit. Back to abnormal. The only difference was that for a brief period Billy Sherrill had a functional alcoholic/cokehead to work with. He took advantage.

George showed up at the Quonset Hut on January 18, 1980, to cut at least his side of "Two Story House," a duet with Tammy. (Tammy normally overdubbed their duets.)

"Women down through the ages have gone crazy trying to harmonize with him," said Sherrill. "They get something right, they get it perfect, he changes it every time. He used to wear Tammy out, trying to phrase with him."

George showed for two back-to-back sessions on January 21, according to Bob Moore's work diary, and at 2 p.m. on February 6, according to the American Federation of Musicians "phonograph recording contract," George came to the studio to work on Master no. NCO 130551, better known as "He Stopped Loving Her Today."

It was a long time coming.

"Once he got the real melody, then we had to wait 'til his voice was able to sing it," recalled Sherrill. "And so he'd come in on a good day—most of them bad days—and try it—no good, no good. So finally one day he came in and he sounded real good. He had a glass of honey and some lemons and did the verses."

They worked on two additional songs during the session: "A Hard Act to Follow" (the flip side of "He Stopped Loving Her Today") and a song that was listed as "The Garage Sale" but was apparently "Garage Sale Today," the flip side of the "I'm Not Ready Yet" single that would be released in August 1980. The paperwork doesn't spell out exactly what was done at any of the sessions, so there's no record of when George finally nailed the recitation, the new spoken, she-came-to-see-him-one-last-time verse.

Bobby Braddock and Curly Putman had expected George would sing the new verse—"They wrote it as a melody," said Billy Sherrill—but Billy had other ideas.

(Why'd you decide to do it as a recitation?)

"It got kinda boring by then. It was a real break in the mood of the song for him to talk, a little bit more dramatic in the middle of the record, just to take a deep breath and talk, instead of sing the whole thing through."

Bad idea. While George could sing fine when he was drunk (often better, actually), he couldn't talk straight. Slurred his words. Then there was the "Millie issue."

Millie Kirkham. You may not know the name, but you know the voice. "She can sing higher than anybody on earth," said Sherrill. That high warbling on the front end of "Blue Christmas," the Elvis classic? That's Millie. And on "He Stopped Loving Her Today," the woman singing the "fill" throughout the spoken verse? Millie again.

Millie's story sounds like a silly, girl-makes-good plot out of a thirties musical. She was a secretary at WSM radio who just happened to sing in the company glee club. This led to radio gigs and a slot with the Anita Kerr Singers. Next up, Elvis, as Millie became a preferred backup singer for The King himself. Not bad for a working mother in the fifties.

"I can remember one time we recorded 'til the sun was coming up and (chuckle) I said, 'Elvis, I gotta go home and get my kids off to school,'" recalled Millie. "'Okay.' He said, 'If we're still going, come on back.'"

For "He Stopped Loving Her Today," recalled Millie, "We did the [tracking] session and then later they called and said, 'Can y'all come over and do some overdubs on it?'" So Millie again joined George, Billy, and the Jordanaires in the studio. And that's the session when she probably did the "wails" for the recitation, a handful of notes that preceded each of the four new lines.

"First time she did it, she did it an octave higher than that which was awful, sounded like a bird or something," recalled

Sherrill. "And I said, 'Please, Millie drop it an octave, where real people sing.' And once she did, it sounded real good."

In Millie's recollection, she was the one worried doing it "up high" would be "a little too brassy sounding," thinking it needed "something a little more mournful sounding."

"I said, 'Let me do it an octave lower and see how you like it.' I said, 'If you don't like it, then I'll go up and do it an octave higher,'" recalled Millie.

She only remembers doing it the one time. George? That was another story. When he attempted to do the overdub with Millie's prerecorded track playing, he couldn't get the timing right.

"I finally got him to wait where she could sing and he could talk and she could sing, 'ooh, ooh,' then he'd talk," said Sherrill. "'Cause he was talking over her. He had it all said a third of the way through what he was supposed to say. He just rattled it off. Finally he got the gist of how to do it. And that came off good. And that was about eight months after he sang the first verse."

"So finally he came in one day and we spent—I dunno—about an hour, which should have taken about eight seconds," continued Sherrill, and finally got it right. That done, "he left again."

Time to add a couple of dollops of the Nashville Sound. On March 5, 1980, composer/arranger Bill McElhiney sweetened things up, overdubbing strings—cellos, violins, and violas, ten in all—onto "He Stopped Loving Her Today." In the finished recording, these violins from hell, actually it was the Sheldon Kurland Strings (Yes, Sheldon is Bluebird Cafe creator Amy Kurland's father), came in at the beginning of the second verse, were joined by the "mooing vocal choruses" for the second half of the verse, and then both continued through to the end of the song.

"Bill McElhiney wrote some fantastic violins on this thing. And where he did the 'glisses' at the end? They didn't like that at the label," said Sherrill. "They said, 'Why'd you raise all those violins?' They always said that."

("Glissando," or "gliss," is music lingo for the violins quickly sawing their way up or down a scale.)

"The string players ran through it and we sat in the control room and listened to it and one change that Billy made turned out to be a brilliant change as far as the string arrangement goes," recalled engineer Ron "Snake" Reynolds. "Right at the first of the chorus, there's a 'glissando,' what they call a 'glissando,' on the strings. Well, Bill [McElhiney] had written it fairly short which would sorta be your standard way to do it. And Billy said, 'No, no. Double it.' So it's a real long build-up. A real long climb on the strings. And that was sort of a signature part of that, part of that record, musically anyway. That was Billy's idea to do that."

Why all the glisses?

"It's like the soul leaving and going to heaven," said Sherrill.

The critics didn't see it that way. Oh they agreed there was a soul leaving, all right, but it didn't belong to the dead man, it belonged to Sherrill and it was heading in quite the opposite direction.

19

EYEWITNESSES V. PAPERWORK

In a town then known for routinely cranking out three songs in one four-hour session, the time it took to produce "He Stopped Loving Her Today" was headline news.

"Eighteen months," wrote Jones in his autobiography. "Over a year," Sherrill told Jones biographer Dolly Carlisle. "A year and a week," said engineer Ron "Snake" Reynolds. But the paperwork on file at Sony contradicts these eyewitness accounts. The paperwork says the production of "He Stopped Loving Her Today" took as little as a month. So which is right?

Here's some of the most compelling testimony that the eyewitnesses, not the paperwork, might have it right. First, Billy Sherrill.

(So if I'm listening to the record, I'm hearing something that was done in '78, and then I'm hearing something that was done in '79.)

"Correct," replied Billy Sherrill.

(And then I'm hearing something that was done in '80?)

"Probably."

Second, engineer Ron "Snake" Reynolds.

(Billy said the thing was really pieced together.)

"Yes."

(That part of the song was cut maybe as early as 1978 and the last of it was cut in early 1980.)

"Yeah."

(So how many sessions are we talking about?)

"You got the basic rhythm track session, you got the string overdub session, and you got the remix session—that's three sessions. Then you got all the vocal sessions," said Reynolds. "Him singing, we probably, oh, did a couple of dozen times where he'd come in and try to sing through the years."

(How many pieces you think that vocal is made up of?)

"Oh, well, like I say, it took over a year, I think it was a year and a week it took to do the vocal. So there might be, y'know, a word, two words, three words from—that are a year old, y'know. Who knows?"

So according to these eyewitnesses, a totally wrecked, snorting and guzzling George Jones was in and out of the studio for a year or more in an epic struggle to produce a serviceable rendition of "He Stopped Loving Her Today." Finally, after another three-week stay at "La-Di-La Acres" in Birmingham, George came up for air and Sherrill and friends pieced together the finished recording in early 1980.

Now for the paperwork. The old CBS/Epic files are now in the care of Sony BMG Nashville and one of Sony's star writers, Bobby Braddock, got the folks at Sony to go through the files for me. Word came on May 30, 2008.

"An exhaustive search" of the archives, emailed Alison Booth, senior director of A&R administration at Sony BMG Nashville, showed that the first time anybody did anything in the studio for "He Stopped Loving Her Today," was not in 1978 or 1979 but on February 6, 1980. Alison had five separate documents showing there was a George Jones session that day (contracts from two different unions, a CBS session data sheet, a copyright clearance form, and the release notice for the album). But most importantly, she had the testimony of Margie Hunt, a CBS executive from the era, who said the particular way the paperwork was filled out, using a CBS internal numbering system, proved that the February 6, 1980, date was indeed the first tracking session for the song. First tracking sessions are the beginning point for virtually all recordings. The instrumental tracks recorded during that session are what the singer sings along with while perfecting the vocal.

The Sony BMG records showed three more sessions where work was done on "He Stopped Loving Her Today": a vocal overdub session on March 3, 1980 (when Millie probably did her thing); a string overdub session on March 5, 1980; and a remix session on March 6, 1980. So according to the Sony BMG paperwork, "He Stopped Loving Her Today" took a month, not a year, to produce. The single was released on April 12, 1980.

"What I have are official paper documents, signed off on by record company staff," emailed Alison Booth. "Time can change memories, but not the paperwork."

So there is no paperwork to support the eyewitness testimony that the song took a year or more to produce. Nada. Zilch.

"I'm sorry I can't make the paperwork match the memories," wrote Alison.

Me too. Having taken the eyewitness accounts as gospel for a couple of years, my first reaction to Alison's news was disbelief: somebody must have monkeyed with the paperwork. Who knows why. Alison didn't think so. And neither did I after Bobby Braddock and guitarist Pete Wade shared their own personal paperwork. First Wade.

Wade's work diary, a record of every session he ever worked (which is totally independent of the Sony BMG paperwork) also shows the first tracking session for "He Stopped Loving Her Today"—the session where he wrote down the chart for the song—came on February 6, 1980.

Bobby Braddock's journal contains a running history of the song. According to that document, he and Curly Putman finished writing "He Stopped Loving Her Today" on October 18, 1977, Braddock cut the demo two days later, and about a year later, on November 27, 1978 (after Johnny Russell's failed attempts), Sherrill told Bobby that George Jones was going to cut the song. About a year after that, on January 17, 1980, Billy told Braddock that "if he [George] showed up the next day and wasn't screwed up on booze and cocaine, they would cut 'He Stopped Loving Her Today.'" George made it to the session in working order (this is the same session where he cut his part of the duet "Two Story House" with Tammy), but, according to the journal, Billy would decide not to cut "He Stopped Loving Her Today" pending revisions. Bobby first sent Billy the rewrite he and Curly had done for Johnny Russell. No sale. Several weeks later, on Tuesday, February 5, Bobby's journal noted he had run "back and forth between

Tree [publishing] and Billy's office in the snow" until he and Curly finally came up with the four-line verse "that Billy deemed 'perfect.'" (So it turns out the long, tortuous rewrites of legend actually only took twenty days.) George would cut the song the next day, February 6, 1980—just like the Sony BMG paperwork said. The day after that Bobby got word "that George Jones was in great voice and 'He Stopped Loving Her Today' came off super."

So is the Sony BMG/Pete Wade/Bobby Braddock timeline right? Could the whole song really have taken only a month to produce beginning with the first tracking session on February 6, 1980? I checked back in with Billy Sherrill.

"I know what they say about tracking and a month—all that— is not right," insisted Billy. "In fact, from the time he did the first verse 'til the time he did the recitation was a year."

On Sherrill's behalf, this is the same story he has been telling to whoever asked for more than twenty years. For example, in *Ragged But Right*, the Jones biography published in 1984, only four years after the song's release when his memory was relatively fresh, Sherrill told author Dolly Carlisle, "It took over a year to record that song."

I went through the Sony BMG timeline with engineer Ron "Snake" Reynolds who handled the string session and most of George's overdubs. "Tracked on February 6," I said. "Released on April 12."

"February, March, April. Aaah. Something don't work out there. Somethin's wrong," said Reynolds. "But Lou [Bradley] would be better able to tell you when it was cut."

I persist.

(If someone were to ask you, "What degree of certainty you had it took more than two months?" What would you say to that?)

"I would have to give way to somebody else's memory," replied Reynolds. "At my age, sixty three, I don't remember yesterday too well. But I do remember it taking a long time. If I had to bet, I'd bet it took more than two months."

I called engineer Lou Bradley again.

(Everybody that actually worked on the record says it took about a year to record "He Stopped Loving Her Today" because

George was having troubles. However, the paperwork kept on file over at Sony from CBS says it only took a couple of months to do it.)

"That, that's more correct," said Bradley.

(Oh, it's correct?)

"Yeah."

(Okay.)

"I did the original tracks—that's my involvement," said Bradley. "I did the live session. And it seems like I did one overdub with George."

"Myths arise, y'know," continued Bradley, chuckling. "Several months turns into six or whatever."

I wondered out loud if there were something going on that was not showing up in the paperwork.

"Well now, that's, that's entirely possible," said Bradley.

There was one piece of evidence coming out of Sony BMG that actually supported the took-a-year scenario, but it's way shaky. After the "exhaustive search" of the archives left me confused, I asked Alison Booth if she would get somebody to take a look at the master tapes themselves that are in storage at Sony's Iron Mountain facility in New York state. What they found was confusing. "Songs recorded on the same day do not appear on the same roll of tape," said Alison's email, and on one tape the songs were not in chronological order by recording date. So Alison concluded that "nothing definitive and without question can be gleaned directly from the tape boxes."

But while the tape boxes themselves were of little help, they did find something of interest inside: a strip of masking tape that had been stuck to the mixing board, the console, in the Quonset Hut control room during the recording session. That masking tape showed what (if anything) was on each of the twenty-four tracks during the first tracking session for "He Stopped Loving Her Today." An engineer "handwrote the track or number on the tape along with instrument names for easy reference. On this particular recording, track one was bass, track two was bass drums, [etc.]." Okay, here's the punch line: that strip of masking tape "shows a date of 2/6/79 for 'He Stopped Loving Her Today,'" wrote Alison.

Note that's *1979*, not 1980. If correct, that would mean "He Stopped Loving Her Today" did take about a year to produce (from February 1979 to March 1980). But Alison thinks the date is wrong; that a mistake was made; that "the engineer that noted the date was still used to writing 1979" that early in 1980.

Maybe.

"We haven't located anything in the files that corresponds to a recording date of 2/6/79," wrote Alison. However, as was noted earlier, there is lots of paperwork showing there was a session a year later on 2/6/80.

Summing up, we have the testimony of eyewitnesses George and Billy and Snake and that strip of masking tape to support the "took-a-year" side and the Sony BMG paperwork, Pete Wade's diary, Bobby Braddock's journal, and the testimony of engineer Lou Bradley to support the "took-a-month" side. Try sorting that out. Why should we care?

First off, like Alison observed, "The memories do make for what is probably a much more interesting story." Who doesn't love to hear about another one of George's epic struggles?

Second, in a book pretty much built around the making of one song, one would think the author would, at a minimum, be able to figure out for certain who played on the damn record and when the damn thing was recorded. One would think. But there is no hope for that unless the Sony BMG paperwork is right. If the first tracking session really came on February 6, 1980, like the Sony BMG records show, then I know exactly who played on the record. I'm sitting here right now looking at the American Federation of Musicians phonograph recording contract for February 6, 1980. I mean, I have their signatures and Social Security numbers: Pete Drake (steel), Bob Moore (bass), Pig Robbins (piano), Billy Sanford (guitar), Pete Wade (guitar), Jerry Carrigan (drums), Charles McCoy (harmonica), Philip Baugh (guitar).

Trouble is, I find both the paperwork from Sony BMG, Pete, and Bobby and the eyewitness testimony from Billy and Snake equally credible. (Then cokehead George, I ain't so sure about.) So I do believe something went on with George and Billy and "He Stopped Loving Her Today" between the time Billy committed to cutting the song in late 1978 and when they finally got around to doing it in February 1980. What exactly is open to speculation. Here's Bobby Braddock's take.

> I can only conclude that the references—made by Billy, George, and the engineer—about "He Stopped Loving Her Today" being initially cut a year before, must pertain to some session the previous year that they cut it, but it didn't come off or George was drunk, and they never made any mention of it to us. It may not have even found its way to a tracking sheet or log book. What eventually came out had to be from the 1980 session because that was the new, longer version, the one with the extra [spoken] verse.

Was the February 6, 1980, session a redo, as Braddock speculates? Bad things have been known to happen to good recordings. Engineer Lou Bradley tells a horror story about Merle Haggard and the making of his 1973 classic "If We Make It Through December." Seems Haggard's first version of the song got lost in the mail somewhere between Nashville and California. The second got erased. Then he came into Lou's studio, the Quonset Hut, and recorded it a third time—one take, no less—and the tape turned out to be defective.

Snake bit.

So I asked Bradley, the lead Quonset Hut engineer, if there were any chance they had to do a second tracking session for "He Stopped Loving Her Today."

"No!" said Bradley.

I asked Sherrill if George could have done "vocals before you did the tracking session?"

"No. No. That would be impossible," said Billy. "He couldn't do vocals without tracks."

So there you have it. In the end, whether you believe the paperwork—it took a month—or the eyewitness accounts— it took a year—may depend on whether you are more likely to believe a first-person narrative spiked with telling details that if not true, ought to be (George kept confusing the melody with "Help Me Make It Through the Night"; could sing drunk, but couldn't get through the recitation without slurring his words;

soothed his throat with honey and lemons) or are more likely to believe what you see in black and white. I don't know what to tell you. For me, it's a tossup, an impasse, a stalemate. Despite my promise, I just haven't been able to sort it out. So, like I told Alison over at Sony, it's probably time for me "to admit to being stumped and get on with my life."

20

COLLABORATION AND COMPILATION

Here I come to save the day!
—MIGHTY MOUSE

Why do we capitalize the word "I"? There's no gram-
matical reason for doing so, and oddly enough, the
majuscule [capital letter] "I" appears only in English.
—CAROLINE WINTER, *New York Times Magazine*

Now back to the big picture. Whether "He Stopped Loving Her Today" took a month or a year to produce, the finished recording ended up being a collaboration—like most recordings. To make the greatest country record of all time, George Jones needed Billy Sherrill who needed Pig Robbins who needed Ron "Snake" Reynolds who needed Charlie McCoy who needed Millie Kirkham who needed Bobby Braddock and Curly Putman who needed Jerry Carrigan and on and on. Like Hillary said, "It takes a village."

"I think toward the end when they're all playing is one of those strange blessings you get when everybody's playing and nobody's clashing with each other," said Sherrill. "Everybody in the record was complementing the other person. And they were all complementing Jones."

A collaboration.

Second, "He Stopped Loving Her Today," like most record-ings, was a compilation of musical elements, a sound mosaic cre-ated in the studio by Billy Sherrill and the engineers.

"Virtually all recorded music is the product of studio manip-ulation," wrote *New York Times* reporter Jon Pareles. "Classical albums are typically pieced together from the best of multiple takes of a work; even live albums, classical and popular, are often

patched up to correct wrong notes. Most popular music is created on multi-track tape that allows dozens of separate elements
to be perfected and combined."

(How did you do that?)

"Back then, you just punch in on tracks," said engineer Ron
"Snake" Reynolds. "You take this track over here you got and
you'll take and lift a sequence out of that, punch it in to another
track where another vocal is. And you go on down a little ways
and you take another track, punch into that track."

"You make what was called then, and still is, I guess, a 'comp
track,'" continued Reynolds. "It's a compilation vocal track. You
get this one master track you're working with and he may come
in and sing next month and we'll pull a line out of that and put it
in that comp track."

Mind you all this punching was done by hand and required
a certain amount of manual dexterity. "You had to be quick," said
Reynolds.

So the songs we love were and are most often created from
pieces—parts, a little of this and a little of that, all assembled—
"perfected and combined"—in the final mix by the producer and
engineers.

So how long does it take to put everything together, to mix
an average song?

"Anywhere from an hour-and-a-half to three hours to mix a
record for us old school guys," said Reynolds. "Some of the new
school guys will take a day or so, or even longer."

"There are some really bizarre stories, like Mutt Lang [Sha-
nia Twain's then producer-husband] and Shania Twain," continued Reynolds. "It took 'em six weeks to mix ten songs."

Once the compilation is done, what you end up with is the
illusion of a continuous, spontaneous performance. An "illusion"
because the song as heard on the recording was never performed
live in quite the same way.

This whole collaboration/compilation thing is hard to get
a handle on. We Americans love our heroes. We want stars to
worship, celebrate, and, yes, write about. That's how the stories
get told. Did you hear the one about the brash young singer-
songwriter who battled Music Row, country radio, Big Foot, and

the Loch Ness Monster before getting her groundbreaking new single out to an adoring public? The very American emphasis on individual achievement, the prototypical one-mouse-can-make-a-difference, "here-I-come-to-save-the-day" story is such an established and powerful cliché that it's almost like we're programmed to believe it.

But the truth is Ben Franklin didn't discover electricity and Edison didn't invent the light bulb. The word "electric" was coined more than a century before Franklin was even born and that kite thing, if it really happened, likely would have lit him up like a Christmas tree. As for the invention of the light bulb, Edison "was not a solitary inventor working in his basement. He had a large staff and organization to carry out his experiments," said ushistory.net.

It was a collaboration.

Likewise recordings aren't made by individuals. They're made by groups and we're not talking the Beatles and the Rolling Stones. We're talking songwriters, producers, session musicians, background singers, and engineers.

So it's time to update the popular notion of what generally goes on in the studio. A great recording is not made by capturing an individual bravura performance on tape. Rather, a great recording is made by compiling a series of pieces created by a collaboration of talented performers.

As for "He Stopped Loving Her Today," when everybody was done playing and singing, overdubbing and glissandoing, Sherrill and the engineers took the raw ingredients and blended them to create the finished product. This recording I first thought was a one- or maybe a two-man tour de force by George Jones and Billy Sherrill was actually an ensemble production. The skills I thought were at work, the skills of soloists, were actually the skills of collaborators and compilers. What I thought I was hearing, a solitary George Jones pouring out his heart in a song, is really the work of a roomful of hearts in emotional sync. It's still art. It's just not a one-man show. It's a team thing. No Mighty Mouse in sight. For me, at least, this is an idea that's going to take a lot of getting used to.

I'm not alone. In most of what you see in print about the music business, there is seldom even a hint at all the collaborating and compiling that goes on. Instead the focus is on individual singers at the expense of songwriters, producers, session musicians, and engineers.

This focus on stars can be traced to label marketing departments. No big surprise. Given the choice of putting a group photo of a dozen, gnarly, behind-the-scenes contributors on the cover of a CD or a photogenic Taylor Swift or Brad Paisley, what would you do? That being said, when the marketing is done and the history is being written, it's time to give everybody their due, including the session musicians, whether the A Team in Nashville, the Funk Brothers in Detroit, or the Wrecking Crew in Los Angeles.

"We all knew the scam that the record companies perpetrated," Los Angeles bass player Carol Kaye said of the labels' failure to credit the Wrecking Crew for playing on records by everyone from the Beach Boys to Simon and Garfunkel. This in an interview with Kent Hartman at AmericanHeritage.com.

"Preserving the illusion that famous bands played their own instruments was big business, very big business," wrote Hartman.

So the labels let us believe that it was one of the Beach Boys and not then unknown Wrecking Crew guitarist Glen Campbell who played on "I Get Around." Again, not a surprise. It's showbiz, baby, and it's the job of the marketing folk to call a carrot a turnip if it will sell another record. So don't blame the labels for not letting us in on the collaborating/compiling secret. Blame the journalists and historians who take the marketing bull at face value and look the other way, sometimes to lethal effect.

• • •

These days it's not uncommon for a pop artist to sing in the studio and lip sync on stage. (See Spears, Britney; Simpson, Ashlee.) But back in the late eighties, Milli Vanilli didn't even live up to that standard. You remember Milli Vanilli, A.K.A. Rob Pilatus and Fabrice Morvan. Those two charismatic, young and pretty, model-handsome, dreadlocked black guys from Europe didn't sing at all. Not in the studio. Not on stage. Rather, the duo lip-synched to recordings cut by three other black guys who weren't so young and pretty.

With Rob and Fab out front, Milli Vanilli sold thirty million singles and eleven million albums, and took home a Grammy for Best New Artist of 1989, before being outed. Savaged by the fans and media, they were eventually forced to return the Grammy and, by the end of 1990, their career was over.

What a crock.

Critics who pretend it was all about the music and that the way-charismatic Rob and Fab weren't an important apart of Milli Vanilli's success are being coy. Milli Vanilli was a collaboration. The dudes didn't sing? That wasn't their job. Rob and Fab essentially were actors cast as "Milli Vanilli: Fabulous Pop Duo." How good were they? Well, they were good enough to fool the fans. They were good enough to fool the media. And, although there were suspicions, they were good enough to fool the music industry pros, their supposed peers, who did the voting for the Best New Artist Grammy in 1989.

That good.

And Rob and Fab should get long overdue credit for that. And the producer, the actual singers, the session musicians, and engineers should all get credit for their contributions. Milli Vanilli was a collaboration. No one person can take credit. No one person can escape blame.

A collaboration.

A lot of heartache could have been avoided in the Milli Vanilli adventure if everybody had just admitted to the collaborative nature of the business from the get go. And I'm not kidding about the heartache. Rob Pilatus got the worst of it. He tried to kill himself in the early nineties and ended up dying of a drug overdose in 1998. That bad.

> So what effect has capitalizing "I" but not "you"—or any other pronoun—had on English speakers? It's impossible to know, but perhaps our individualistic, workaholic society would be more rooted on community and quality and less focused on money and success if we each thought of our selves as a small "i" with a sweet little dot.
>
> —CAROLINE WINTER, *New York Times Magazine*

March 10, 1980. Mixing done, it was time to share the latest Sherrill/Jones et al. collaboration/compilation, "He Stopped Loving Her Today."

"When he [Sherrill] got finished he called Dan Wilson and Bobby and myself over to hear it," recalled song co-writer Curly Putman. (Wilson was the song plugger from Tree Publishing.)

"He called us over to hear it and we just, uh, I mean it knocked us all out when he played it. He was thrilled with it too," said Putman.

"I think 'He Stopped Loving Her Today' was an okay song," said Bobby Braddock. "But I think Billy Sherrill's production and George Jones singing of it, rendering of it, made it the standard that it is. When I went to hear the cut on it, it wasn't a song I was all that keen on. Billy played me his cut and I thought, 'Holy smokes, man.' I just—I knew, I knew, I'd just heard something very, very special."

"I certainly don't think that's the best country song ever written. Though a lot of people have said that, I don't believe that at all," continued Braddock. "The whole thing's totally subjective, but that certainly is a good candidate for the best country *record* ever made."

Sherrill would play it for George. "I said, 'We got a record here, Jones.'" If Billy was fishing for a compliment, he didn't get one.

"I looked Billy square in the eye and said 'Nobody will buy that morbid son of a bitch,'" recalled George in his autobiography. "Then I marched out the door."

"That's the last words he said," recalled Billy, laughing. "I said. 'They may not buy it, but they're gonna have the opportunity.'"

Sherrill would "bet him [George] a hundred bucks it would go to number one," reported Jones biographer Bob Allen, and that paid off. "He Stopped Loving Her Today" was released on April 12, 1980, and stayed on the charts for eighteen weeks, reaching number one in early July. It was George's first number one solo hit in almost six years. The single of "He Stopped Loving Her Today" would sell over a million copies and be named CMA Single of the Year in 1980. It would earn Bobby Braddock and

Curly Putman the CMA award for Song of the Year in both 1980 and 1981; Jones the CMA award for Male Vocalist of the Year in both 1980 and 1981; and Jones a Grammy for Best Country Vocal Performance, Male in 1980.

"I've had my share of career records," wrote Jones in his autobiography. "'He Stopped Loving Her Today' did more for my career than all of the others combined."

"To put it simply, I was back on top," wrote Jones. "A four-decade career had been salvaged by a three minute song."

Three minutes, fifteen seconds to be exact.

"When this record hit, it was like a rebirth of Jones's confidence," said Billy Sherrill, "confidence in himself."

(The single?)

"Yeah. Then it got easier to say, 'Jones, y'know, come on in, man,'" and Jones was soon back at the Quonset Hut.

In those days when a label had a smash hit, "the monster greed" took over and the label was soon demanding, "Get us an album! Get us an album!" Sherrill told the *Journal of Country Music* in 1978. *I Am What I Am* would turn out to be one of George's best albums ever, yielding two more classics: "If Drinkin' Don't Kill Me (Her Memory Will)" (Harlan Sanders/Richard Beresford) and Tom T. Hall's "I'm Not Ready Yet." But "He Stopped Loving Her Today" was the song that got 'em going out on the road. "They go crazy when I sing that song," Jones told Sherrill. There were some other folks who went crazy over the song, but not in a good way.

Critics had jumped Sherrill in the past when, as scholar Charles Wolfe phrased it in *The Illustrated History of Country Music*, he "would occasionally saddle Jones with strings and background choirs." Ditto for "He Stopped Loving Her Today."

Billy had never been popular with critics. First, he was crazy successful, which is generally a no-no (success and art being mutually exclusive, after all). Second, he was a world-class smartass, and third, he embraced the Nashville Sound, leading to an unholy reliance on the "violins from hell" and "mooing vocal choruses" in his Countrypolitan productions. It was enough to get Jones biographer Bob Allen all riled up.

"Because of his overbearing tendency to bury the fiery heart and soul of traditional hard-core country and honky tonk sound beneath an urbane gruel of gushing vocal harmonies and double-track string orchestras, Sherrill came to be regarded in more conservative-minded circles as nothing less than a pariah," wrote Allen in his 1984 biography of Jones.

"[To those conservatives] his overwrought, pop-influenced production innovations were about as welcome in Nashville as a cholera epidemic," Allen continued.

Sherrill became a carrier, infecting one hit record after another with elements of the dread Nashville Sound. None of this criticism fazed Sherrill. He not only didn't apologize for "diluting" country music (as Chet Atkins tended to do), but was more than happy to take the rap for the strings and the vocals. "I don't think you're losing anything. I think you're gaining something," he told Charles Wolfe. Still, it's not like Sherrill was the first to saddle Jones with either strings or background singers.

In the liner notes to *The Essential George Jones*, Rich Kienzle mentions "a vocal chorus" in the "Tender Years" (1961) and, in that same collection, you also can hear a "vocal chorus" on "The Window Up Above" released a year earlier. All this about a decade before Jones hooked up with Sherrill. So what about strings? Was Billy Sherrill really the first to use the violins from hell on a Jones record?

Not wanting to spend more than about two minutes researching this heady topic, I went straight to YouTube to hear George's "Mockingbird Hill," one of sixteen duets he cut with Gene Pitney in the mid-sixties. (Four of these actually made the charts.) The hunch paid off. There were strings all over the place on that one and on a second Jones-Pitney duet, "I'm a Fool To Care." The point: five years before he hooked up with Sherrill, Jones was at least tolerating strings.

"It was not only the reviewers that did that" ["whupped up on" him for using strings], Sherrill told author Michael Kosser. "The first call I got on 'He Stopped Loving Her Today' was from the label. 'Why did you have to put all those damned violins swirling around?' I said, 'Because the record called for it!'"

"You can't worry about what anybody says," Sherrill told me. "You start worrying about what people say, you change your way of doing things. At that point in my career at Epic, I didn't care whether they liked it—I put out a lot of stuff they didn't like that were hits."

While Sherrill spent the better part of his career taking body blows from critics for "bland, easy-going, easy-listening music," and "slick, cream-puff arrangements," as Wolfe phrased it, George and Tammy were the Teflon twosome. Nothing stuck. Anything on a record that critics didn't like was all the fault of the evil Svengali, Billy Sherrill.

"They would have been so beautiful, pure country if he hadn't of put all those mushy, mushy strings around them, all those voices, all this and all that," said Sherrill. "Don't bother me."

As for the purists out there, said Sherrill, "If you could put strings on one of their things to make it go to number one, you've have forty strings on there."

Critic Nick Tosches seconded that in *Where Dead Voices Gather*. "Any primitive-sounding artist, no matter how great his gift or integrity, would gladly, if he could, refine that primatism and adulterate the truth of himself and his voice, to increase the prospect of sales whenever possible. . . . The blues to all who knew and loved them, were far less a god than money."

So what are we to make of George Jones, the man who so famously promised "You're always gonna hear a fiddle on a George Jones record," then went on to sing on dozens of fiddle-free recordings? What are we to make of the man who declared "You don't walk out on stage with a thirty-six piece orchestra if you're gonna sing country music" and then stood still while Billy Sherrill massed strings on his recordings and, more recently, as Paul Shaffer massed violins—I counted ten— for a 2006 performance of "He Stopped Loving Her Today" on the Letterman show? Nick Tosches has a possible explanation. After years of hearing George insist he was "trying to get back to the pure country," and never quite making it, Tosches decided, for Jones, "'pure country' might be the unattainable goal that to some degree kept him moving forward"; the impossible dream;

"a man's reach should exceed his grasp," and all that. Meanwhile, the "lush orchestral arrangements and saccharine background voices," wrote Tosches, would help "keep the singer commercially alive." So Tosches found a way for George to have his violins and keep his country, too.

I thought to just go ahead and ask George face to face if he ever felt the need to, as Tosches put it, "refine [his] primatism and adulterate the truth of himself and his voice, to increase the prospect of sales." Thought to ask how he goes about balancing the "unattainable goals" of art and the necessities of commerce.

Yeah, right.

•   •   •

Today "He Stopped Loving Her Today" is almost universally viewed as the definitive country song, strings and all.

"I think that's the best part of the record," said Bobby Braddock. "It doesn't have to be somebody thumpin' on a washtub to make it country," he continued.

"People were saying that Billy Sherrill had these schlocky arrangements," Braddock said, "and did something detrimental to country music. The truth of the matter is, you look back on it, a historical perspective, Billy Sherrill produced some of the greatest traditional country records of our time."

Songs like "He Stopped Loving Her Today," "Stand By Your Man," "D-I-V-O-R-C-E," "If Drinkin' Don't Kill Me (Her Memory Will)," "Still Doin' Time," "I Always Get Lucky With You," "Take This Job and Shove It," et cetera, ad infinitum.

"Billy Sherrill's a genius," continued Braddock. "He and Owen Bradley tower over all the rest. . . . He put his fingerprints on everything he did. He had his own sound. . . . I think he took a lot of the really traditional country stuff and made it very accessible."

In a weak moment, even Sherrill admitted there might be something about "He Stopped Loving Her Today" that mattered more than what it did for his bank account.

"You get kind of a proud and eternal type feeling knowing that they'll be doing this after you're dead," said Billy. "I guess knowing it'll be around after you die is probably the best feeling."

Not that he plans on giving up the house boat.

. . .

George had just two lines to sing when Barbara Mandrell approached him in the audience at the 1981 CMA Awards. Just like on her record, he was to chime in on the chorus of "I Was Country When Country Wasn't Cool": "I was country when country wasn't cool. / Yeah, I was country from my hat down to my boots."

"I couldn't remember one word," wrote George in his autobiography. "I fumbled and mumbled."

George had shown up drunk and not only did he muff the Barbara Mandrell song, show producers had to cancel his planned performance of "He Stopped Loving Her Today." Good thing. It was all George could do to make it to the stage to pick up his award for Male Vocalist of the Year, where he thanked country music pioneers Johnny Wright and Kitty Wells. Why? Blinded by the TV lights, "they were the only people I could see," said George.

And what was Jones's punishment for embarrassing himself and his label in front of the whole world? A new half-million-dollar contract with CBS including a hundred thousand dollars in cash which he quickly blew on "a new Corvette, a lot of cocaine," and "foolishness." A month later, Jones's newfound success would lead to a blind date with Nancy Sepulvado, a telephone assembly line worker from Shreveport, Louisiana. It would take a while, but this liaison would change George's life forever.

"Nancy came along. And she turned him around. She straightened him out, cleaned him up, got him off that junk," said Billy Sherrill. "And that was the biggest turnaround in his life. She gets the credit for that. She's something else."

Nancy took over management of George's career in 1982, the same year he finally kicked cocaine, and they married in March 1983. George had given up coke following a thirty-day stay at Hill Crest in Birmingham, where he actually was scoring the drug inside the hospital. He got caught, they kicked him out, and George came straight home, took one last snort from a stash stored in the freezer, and, suddenly, "the craving was gone," wrote George in his autobiography. "The stuff suddenly sickened me."

The booze? That would take a little longer. George would claim he quit drinking for good sometime in 1986. Me, I'm inclined to think it was at around 1:30 p.m. on Saturday, March 6, 1999.

• • •

The first call from his SUV was to Ellen Shriver at Bandit Records.

"He was listening to seven songs he had recorded," reported the *Tennessean*, "and was so excited he wanted to play them for her over the phone, but could not get his cassette player to work."

The second call was home to tell them he was on his way.

"'Oh my God!' were the last words legendary country singer George Jones spoke into his cellular telephone just before his luxury sports-utility vehicle slammed into a concrete bridge abutment," said the *Tennessean* account of the accident.

This on a two-lane road close to Jones's home in Franklin, Tennessee.

"A bottle of vodka, which had been opened and resealed, was found under the passenger seat in Jones's Lexus," the newspaper would report later.

It took about ninety minutes to free the sixty-seven-year-old singer from the wreckage. He was helicoptered to Vanderbilt hospital in Nashville suffering from a lacerated liver, collapsed lung, and internal bleeding.

"It looked to me like he was at death's door," the Vanderbilt emergency room surgeon told the *Tennessean*. "It's remarkable that he's alive at this point."

George spent two weeks in the hospital and two months later pled guilty to DUI charges and apologized for his actions.

"I don't remember much about the day of the accident, but I do know I was drinking and obviously my driving was impaired,"

Jones told the media. "I did wrong that day and I take full responsibility for what happened. I've had a life of long struggle with alcohol and I thought I had won since I had been sober for more than twelve years."

"Truthfully, the struggle never ends," George continued, "and I will get treatment to help me cope better."

From all reports, George has been sober ever since.

EPILOGUE
True Love Purgatory

George Jones's "He Stopped Loving Her Today" makes you, too, want
to love someone so hard that you won't quit 'til your breath leaves the
circle of your teeth, just as it makes you long for such a love.
— DAVID KIRBY, *New York Times Book Review*

Sunday, the Ryman Auditorium, downtown Nashville. A gor-
geous spring day, temperature in the seventies.

It had been just shy of three years since last I'd seen George
Jones perform here. Enough time for Sun Trust Bank to erect
a perky, thirteen-story, blue-tinted, glass-and-steel office build-
ing in what had been the Ryman's north parking lot and for the
Baptists to throw up a Bible-toting, larger-than-life statue of Billy
Graham a couple of blocks west. For what that's worth.

The George Jones show wouldn't start for another couple of
hours, but his glistening purple and silver tour buses and two
white Mercedes, NOSHOW II and NOSHOW III, were already
parked out front. Dozens of fans, middle-aged or better, milled
around in the auditorium's cobblestone courtyard, and the concrete benches surrounding the bronze statue of Captain Tom
Ryman were filled with a gaggle of pants-wearing women in comfortable shoes.

I chatted up Charles Frederick, a sixty-something songwriter
(also wearing comfortable shoes) who had driven eleven hours
from West Virginia to see the show. "George is the real deal," he
told me, clutching a pack of Camels. That's what everybody says,
of course: "That George Jones, he's the real deal."

George came on to a standing ovation at 8:32, leading off with the usual, "Why Baby Why?" He had made some changes, though, giving up his guitar—it was little more than a prop anyway—after breaking his wrist. He had also rethought his wardrobe, tossing the ghost-of-Nudie fancy black jacket with sparkling embroidery in favor of simple black pants and shirt with a gray shirt jacket. It was a stripped-down, back-to-basics look.

The toning down of the stage garb fit right into George's no-frills image. Like George told the Ryman audience: "We're traditional country. It's the real stuff." So the more he looked on stage like he looks in real life, the less he seemed to be acting, and the more authentic the performance appeared to be. But really, all this was pretending to not be pretending. Like it or not, George Jones is in the same business as Carrot Top and Lady Gaga, and the Ryman Auditorium is just as much a land of make believe as a Broadway theater and a Hollywood backlot. A stage is a stage is a stage. George *is* a country star and he *was* putting on a show even if his particular shtick is "This is not showbiz, this is the real deal." Why all the denial? Remember the billboard.

AUTHENTICITY
WHAT COUNTRY IS

So authenticity is the standard for a music made in a world of make believe. This means with-it country music fans have to learn to live with cognitive dissonance, a psychological conflict resulting from believing two contradictory ideas at the same time.

"We accept that the actors of stage and film are playing roles, but we often resist admitting that singers do much the same thing," wrote David Cantwell in *Oxford American*. "Actors should be believable, we insist, but singers must be 'authentic.' They must not only seem real, but be real."

• • •

At precisely 8:56 p.m., the battle with the pine pews was lost. My butt was officially numb. It was then George launched into his eighth song of the night, "I'm Not Ready Yet," followed by guest artist Jack Greene, a one-time CMA vocalist of the year, who sang his 1969 hit, "Statue of a Fool." That got a standing ovation. George then sang duets with backup singer Brittany Allyn ("Near You") and opening act Jason Byrd ("Yesterday's Wine"), and brought the house down with a near-perfect rendition of Paul Overstreet's "Same Ole Me." That alone was worth an eleven hour-drive.

The audience would stand and cheer when they heard the opening notes of song number twenty four, "He Stopped Loving Her Today." Then came a continuous murmur as folks did what the announcer had asked them to do before the show, forgo the cigarette lighters, and dig out cell phones to wave over their heads. By the time everybody got that taken care of, the song was better than half over and George had lost his place. All that and George still got a standing ovation. This was, after all, the signature song, sung by the signature singer of country music's first century.

The number one qualification for a great country singer like George Jones has always been authenticity. What's it mean to be authentic? Forget the image, country performers, all performers, are authentic, are the real deal, to the extent they are actually experiencing the emotions they're singing about and are making the audience feel the same thing.

"It's our own responses, finally, that hold the only authenticity that matters," wrote Cantwell in the *Oxford American*.

If a country singer can't move an audience, all the trappings of authenticity don't matter. They can trace their singing styles back to Jimmie, Hank, and George. They can wear the cowboy outfit. They can suffer with the best of them. They can have more country cred than a one-armed, Mississippi sharecropper. But none of that means a thing if they can't deliver the emotional charge that is at the heart of country music.

"He'd give you the shivers, man," engineer Ron "Snake" Reynolds said of George Jones. And this wasn't in some fancy setting, but in a plain-as-Polly studio over on Music Row. "He'd hit some of those licks he hits and send shivers up and down your spine. Even Billy and I and people who were in the control room, who were used to it: it'd give you a charge."

Even in a collaborative world like country music George Jones stands out. So what is it exactly that George does to produce those shivers? Nobody knows, really. You can talk, write, and research yourself silly and still not come up with an answer for that one. He just does.

He's *George Jones*.

• • •

And finally, the song: "He Stopped Loving Her Today." There have been a jillion songs written about lost love over the years. Everything from "Lovesick Blues" to "Whiskey Lullaby." But one, "He Stopped Loving Her Today" [hyperbole alert], has become the universal anthem for anyone who has ever had a broken heart except maybe Bobby Braddock. Remember that remark from Bobby earlier about the character in the song being "a very bad role model" who should have "just moved on." Well, nobody's gonna fight Bobby on that one. But before you, the broken hearted, can go about "living your life," there's a brief time when it's too soon to give up, to admit that the love you thought was "forever and ever, amen" is not "'til death do us part" after all. So for a time (a few weeks, a month, or maybe even a coke-and-booze induced span of years), before you slide the capo of love up the guitar neck of life to "move on" mode, you get to pretend your love really is eternal, like in the fairy tales and romantic comedies. That's the time for "He Stopped Loving Her Today."

The time to wallow.

"I'll love you 'til I die," the man said. And unlike us, he really meant it. Our hero wasn't hooking up with somebody new two weeks after the breakup. He wasn't cruising the nearest meat market. He was home hanging "her picture on the wall," going "half crazy now and then." And long after the love of his life had moved on, perhaps remarried twice, first to "a handsome, young, Nashville real estate broker" and then a Music Row insider, our hero "still loved her through it all, hoping she'd come back again." All that, because love is pretend-eternal during the time of "He Stopped Loving Her Today." There'll be a whole lifetime to give up on that bittersweet notion. Meanwhile, you stay stuck in true-love purgatory, stalling, before you give in to what your head knows all along—vaguely—that, like the woman said, "You'll forget in time." Until then, you pretend dying will be the only cure for this wretched sorrow. Suffer. Enjoy. Yes, *enjoy*. For mercifully, sadly, that feeling of love eternal won't last long.

Oh, by the way, ain't nobody coming back. Not after all this time. You wouldn't want them to anyway. Not really. But for a moment, it's okay to hark back to the olden days when you did. Want them back, I mean. It's easy, like slipping on a pair of old shoes. Slip 'em on, wonder "what if?" Listen to "He Stopped Loving Her Today." Maybe wipe away a tear or two.

And remember.

What they said. What they did.

What *you* said. What *you* did.

SOURCES

"About the Fund." At the Sound Recording Special Payments Fund web site www.sound-recording.org.

Accountant, The. Written and Directed by Ray McKinnon. 38 min. Ginny Mule Pictures, 2001. Film.

Alden, Grant. "Old Wound and the New Right." *No Depression.* March 8, 2006. nodepression.com.

Allen, Nik. "Deliverance Movie." "70's Movies Rewind," 70s.fast-rewind.com.

Allen, Bob. "The Decline and Fall of George Jones." *Country Music,* January–February 1979.

———. *George Jones: The Life and Times of a Honky Tonk Legend.* New York: Birch Lane Press, 1994.

Anderson, Patrick. "The Real Nashville." *New York Times Magazine,* August 31, 1975.

Atkins, Chet. "How Chet Atkins Did It: 1957–74." Transcript of remarks made at the Country Music Foundation, April 20, 1987. In Kingsbury, Paul, ed., *Country: The Music and the Musicians,* 2nd ed., 292–93. New York: Abbeville Press, 1988.

Barker, Hugh, and Yuval Taylor. *Faking It: The Quest for Authenticity in Popular Music.* New York: W.W. Norton, 2007.

Bensman, Marvin R. "The History of Broadcasting: Programs 50s." In "Radio Archive of the University of Memphis" umdrive.memphis.edu/mbensman/public/history1.html.

Bernard, Ryan Carson. "The Rise and Fall of the Hillbilly Music Genre: A History, 1922–39." Masters thesis, East Tennessee State University, December 2006.

"Biography: George Jones: The King of Heartache." Executive producers Craig Haffner and Donna E. Lusitana, 50 min., Greystone Productions for A&E Television Network, 1996, videocassette.

Blume, Jason. *This Business of Songwriting.* New York: Billboard Books, 2006.

Braddock, Bobby, and Claude Putman, Jr. "He Stopped Loving Her Today." Sony/ATV Music Publishing, LLC, 1978.

Brooks, Garth. Blurb for *I Lived to Tell It All.* George Jones with Tom Carter. New York: Dell, 1996.

Brown, Jim. *George Jones: Why Baby Why?* Kingston, Ontario: Quarry Press, 2001.

Campbell, Walter. "Interview: Billy Sherrill." *Journal of Country Music* 7, no. 2 (May 1978).

Cantwell, David. "Sammi Smith: The Art of Authenticity." *Oxford American*, Summer 2005.

Carlisle, Dolly. "The Fall and Rise of George Jones." *Penthouse*, November 1980.

———. *Ragged But Right: The Life and Times of George Jones.* Chicago: Contemporary Books, 1984.

Carr, Patrick. "Will the Circle Be Unbroken: The Changing Image of Country Music." In Kingsbury, *Country: The Music and the Musicians*, 328–59.

Carter, A. P. "Little Darling Pal of Mine." Peer International.

CBS/Epic Phonograph Recording Contracts (Session Sheets) of the American Federation of Musicians Local 257 for 18 January 1980; 6 February 1980; 5 March 1980. On file in the Frist Library and Archive at the Country Music Hall of Fame and Museum in Nashville, TN.

Clarke, Donald. *The Rise and Fall of Popular Music: A Polemical History.* New York: St. Martin's, 1996.

Collings, Matthew, and Ian MacMillan. *It Hurts: New York Art From Warhol to Now.* London: 21 Publishing, 1999.

Collins, Glenn. "Re-creating Hambone, Body Music of the Past." *New York Times*, July 18, 1987.

Cooper, Peter. "Hut's Recording Days Hold Historic Moments." *Tennessean*, 22 January 2005.

———. "Meet the Genius Behind Many a Country Hit." *Tennessean*, August 24, 2008.

Cooper, Peter, and Brad Schmitt. "Country Goes Pop, Stays Traditional." *Tennessean*, 16 November 2005.

Cox, Jim. *Goodnight, Gracie: The Last Years of Network Radio.* Jefferson, NC: McFarland, 2002.

Daley, Dan. "Producer Billy Sherrill." *Mix*, July 2002, mixonline.com.

Dawidoff, Nicholas. *In the Country of Country: A Journey to the Roots of American Music.* New York: Vintage, 1998.

Dean, Eddie. "Nudie and the Technicolor Jacket" jewsrock.com.

Deen, Dixie. "The Crown Prince of C-W Music." *Music City News*, August 1966.

Deliverance. Directed by John Boorman. Warner Bros., 1972. Film.

Dew, Joan. "The George Jones Explosion." *Country Music*, August 1977.

Dickey, James. *Deliverance.* New York: Dell, 1970.

Diebel, Matt. "George's Gems: Is George Jones the Greatest Ever?" *Time*, October 6, 2000.

Dorment, Richard. "The Naked and the Dead." *Daily Telegraph*, June 27, 2006.

East, Jim. "Doctors to Start Weaning Singer Off Respirator." *Tennessean*, March 8, 1999.

———. "Family, Friends, Fans Keep Up With Legend's Condition." *Tennessean*, March 8, 1999.

Eipper, Laura. "George Jones Is Singing a New Song." *Tennessean*, April 6, 1979.

Elliott, Debbie. "A Jazz Guitar Legend: Alive and 75," transcript of interview with Kenny Burrell. *All Things Considered*, July 1, 2007, www.npr.org.

"Encore 54." Produced by Richard Fatherley. Online video of June 11, 2004, conference in commemoration of the 1954 beginnings of Top Forty radio in Kansas City www.archive.org/details/RichardWFatherley.

Farina, Richard. *Been Down So Long It Looks Like Up to Me*. New York: Random House, 1966.

Fields, Arthur, and Walter Donovan. "Aba Daba Honeymoon." Alfred Publishing.

Fisher, Marc. *Something in the Air: Radio, Rock, and the Revolution That Shaped a Generation*. New York: Random House, 2007.

Fleming, Michael. "Universal Sets Up Milli Vanilli Film." *Variety*, February 14, 2007.

Fleming, Kye, and Dennis Morgan. "I Was Country When Country Wasn't Cool." Hall-Clement Publishing.

Fong-Torres, Ben. "Like a Rolling Stone Richard Fatherley Knows Best", www.reelradio.com/storz/index.html.

Friedman, Ted. "Milli Vanilli and the Scapegoating of the Inauthentic." *Bad Subjects*, November 1993 bad.eserver.org/.

Fulford, Robert. "What Is Real Country Music? It's Often Whatever the Latest Musical Generation Says It Is." *National Post*, May 13, 2003 www.robertfulford.com.

"George Jones Enters National Recording Registry." Great American Country website, 10 June 2009 www.gactv.com.

George Jones: Golden Hits. Produced by Dennis M. Hedlund and Gregory Hall. Directed by Mark Hall. 50 min. West Long Branch, NJ: White Star, 2001, DVD.

"George Jones Puts Guitar Aside." http://www.gactv.com, 3 July 2008.

George Jones: Same Ole Me (revised). Produced by Charlie Dick and Gregory Hall. Directed by Mark Hall. 60 min. West Long Branch, NJ: White Star, 2001, DVD.

Goodman, Fred. "Country Radio: Nowhere in New York." *New York Times*, February 16, 2003.

Grady, John. "Dreams, Myths, Facts: The Record Business Today." Notes by author, adult education class, University School, Nashville, TN, January 24, 2006.

Green, Douglas B. "The Road to Nashville." In Carr, Patrick, ed., *The Illustrated History of Country Music*, 164–86. Garden City, NY: Doubleday, 1979.

———. "Tumbling Tumbleweeds: Gene Autry, Bob Wills, and the Dream of the West." In Kingsbury, *Country: The Music and the Musicians*, 78–103.

Green, Douglas B., and Bob Pinson. "Music From the Lone Star State." In Carr, *The Illustrated History of Country Music*, 102–37.

Green, Douglas B., and William Ivey. "The Nashville Sound." In Carr, *The Illustrated History of Country Music*, 238–56.

Guralnick, Peter. *Last Train to Memphis: The Rise of Elvis Presley*. Boston: Back Bay, 1995.

Harkins, Anthony. *Hillbilly: A Cultural History of an American Icon*. Oxford: Oxford University Press, 2004.

Harrington, Jim. "Album Review: George Jones, 'Hits I Missed . . . and One I Didn't.'" Live Daily, 23 September 2005 www.livedaily.com.

Hartman, Kent. "The Wrecking Crew." March 2007 www.americanheritage.com.

Havighurst, Craig. *Air Castle of the South: WSM and the Making of Music City*. Urbana: University of Illinois Press, 2007.

Hendrickson, Lucas. "Tin Pan Shows Country's Backbone." *Tennessean*, April 7, 2005.

"Hoedown on a Harpsichord." *Time*, November 14, 1960.

Hoffman, Al, Bob Merrill, and Clem Watts. "If I Knew You Were Comin,' I'd've Baked a Cake." Colgems-EMI Music, Inc.

Hogeland, William. "Oh Brother: The Bluegrass Purists Don't Understand Country Music. Here's What They're Missing." *Slate*, July 3, 2002 www.slate.msn.com.

———. "The Second Coming of Countrypolitan." *New York Times*, January 2, 2005.

Huey, Steve. "Milli Vanilli: Full Biography." *All Music Guide* www.allmusic.com.

Hughes, Robert. *American Visions: The Epic History of Art in America*. New York: Alfred A. Knopf, 1997.

Ian, Janis. "The Internet Debacle—An Alternative View." *Performing Songwriter*, May 2002.

"Invention of the Lightbulb." www.ushistory.net/electricity.html.

Ivey, Bill. "The Bottom Line: Business Practices That Shaped Country Music." In Kingsbury, *Country: The Music and the Musicians*, 280–311.

———. Review of *Country Music U.S.A.* by Bill C. Malone. In *The Country Reader: Twenty-five Years of the Journal of Country Music*, edited by Paul Kingsbury, 287–90. Nashville and London: Country Music Foundation Press and Vanderbilt University Press, 1996.

Jackson, Alan. Blurb for Jones with Tom Carter, *I Lived to Tell It All*.

Jarnigan, Bill. "'See If Your God Can Save You Now,' George Said as He Pulled the Trigger." *Country Music*, January–February 1979.

Jensen, Joli. "Gender and Recalcitrance: Country Music's Move Uptown." *Tracking: Popular Music Studies* 1, no. 1 (Spring 1988): 30–41.

———. *The Nashville Sound: Authenticity, Commercialization, and Country Music*. Nashville and London: The Country Music Foundation Press and Vanderbilt University Press, 1998.

"Jones, George." *Nashville Banner*, November 22, 1978, notes from *Nashville Banner* morgue now on file at the downtown Nashville Public Library.

"Jones, George." *Nashville Banner*, December 15, 1978, notes from *Nashville Banner* morgue now on file at the downtown Nashville Public Library.

"Jones, George." *The Tennessean*, January 23, 1979, notes from *Nashville Banner* morgue now on file at the downtown Nashville Public Library.

Jones, George. Interview by Charlie Monk, Sirius Satellite Radio, audio tape recording, Nashville, TN, January 25, 2007.

Jones, George, with Tom Carter. *I Lived to Tell It All*. New York: Dell, 1996.

"Joseph P. Webster." Biography of composer of "Wildwood Flower." Walcourt Country Historical Society, Elkhorn, Wisconsin www.geocities.com/walcohistory/webster.

Keel, Beverly. "ACM Red Carpet: Cavalli Popular With Country Stars." *Tennessean*, May 15, 2007.

———. "For Ashley Cleveland It's a Great Time to Be a Woman Who Rocks." *Tennessean*, February 10, 2008.

———. "For Brad Paisley, Success Is Sweet . . . Literally." *Tennessean*, February 15, 2008.

———. "Survival Tactics." *Nashville Scene*, July 15, 1999.

———. "Willie, Kris and Allison Restore My Faith in Music." *Tennessean*, November 11, 2007.

Keillor, Garrison. "Onward and Upward with the Arts at the Opry." *New Yorker*, May 6, 1974.

Keith, Michael C. *Talking Radio: An Oral History of American Radio in the Television Age*. Armonk, NY: M.E. Sharpe, 1999.

"Kesey on LSD." YouTube video from History Channel. July 2, 2006.

Killen, Buddy (with Tom Carter). *By the Seat of My Pants: My Life in Country Music*. New York: Simon and Schuster, 1993.

Kirby, David. "New Hampshire Hoedown." Review of *Sing Me Back Home: Love, Death, and Country Music* by Dana Jennings. *New York Times Book Review*, June 1, 2008.

Klein, Joe. "Forever Weird." Review of *Gonzo: The Life of Hunter S. Thompson* by Jann S. Wenner and Corey Seymour. *New York Times Book Review*, November 18, 2007.

Kosser, Michael. *How Nashville Became Music City, U.S.A.: 50 Years of Music Row*. Milwaukee: Hal Leonard, 2006.

Kristofferson, Kris. "Help Me Make It Through the Night." Combine Music Corporation.

Lilly, John. "Jimmie Rodgers and the Bristol Sessions." In *The Bristol Sessions: Writings About the Big Bang of Country Music*, edited by Charles K. Wolfe and Ted Olson. Jefferson, NC: McFarland, 2005.

Lomax, John III. *Nashville: Music City U.S.A.* New York: Harry N. Abrams, 1985.

Long, Diane, Jim East, and Jennifer Peebles. "George Jones Badly Hurt in Crash." *Tennessean*, March 7, 1999.

Love, Courtney. "Artist Rights and Recording Companies." Letter to recording artists. March 28, 2001. www.gerryhemingway.com.

Lynn, Loretta, with Patsi Bale Cox. *Still Woman Enough: A Memoir*. New York: Hyperion, 2002.

Mabus, Joel. "Performers Column." *Folk Alliance Newsletter*, October 1999 www.joelmabus.com/royalties.htm.

MacDonald, Jay. "Interview: Bobby Braddock," June 18, 2007 //www.bankrate
.com.

Malone, Bill C. *Country Music, U.S.A.*, 2nd ed. Austin: University of Texas
Press, 2002.

Merrill, Bob. "How Much Is That Doggie in the Window?" Alfred Publishing.

Miele, Frank J. J. "National Historic Landmark Nomination: Ryman
Auditorium." Atlanta: National Park Service, 2000.

Morris, Edward. "Country Radio Loves George Jones—In Person." www.cmt
.com/news.

Morthland, John. "Changing Sounds, Changing Methods." *Journal of Country
Music* 12, no. 2 (1989).

Nash, Alanna. *Behind Closed Doors: Talking with the Legends of Country Music.*
New York: Alfred A. Knopf, 1988.

———. "Home Is Where the Gig Is: Life On and Off the Road." In Kingsbury,
Country: The Music and the Musicians, 176–91.

Naujeck, Jeanne Anne. "Sale Could Open Historic Recording Studio to Public."
Tennessean, January 22, 2005.

Nelson, Willie. *Willie: An Autobiography.* Landam, MD: Cooper Square Press,
2000.

"1966 Grammy Award Winners." Hot Pop Songs.com www.hotpopsongs.com.

"Nudie." www.showstudio.com.

"Nudie Cohen: Rodeo Cowboy to the Stars." www.placeboma.com.

Oermann, Robert K. *A Century of Country: An Illustrated History of Country
Music.* New York: TV Books, 1999.

Orbinger, Lee Ann. "How Music Royalties Work." www.howstuffworks.com.

Paducah, Kentucky. City profile material. Gaseous Diffusion Plant www.usec
.com. National Quilt Museum and Artists Relocation Program.
www.paducaharts.com. Demographics. www.city-data.com.

Palmer, Robert. "Nashville Sound: Country Music in Decline." *New York Times*,
September 17, 1985.

Pareles, Jon. "Wages of Silence: Milli Vanilli Loses a Grammy Award." *New York
Times*, November 20, 1990.

Pecknold, Diane. *The Selling Sound: The Rise of the Country Music Industry.*
Durham, NC: Duke University Press, 2007.

Peer, Ralph. "Ralph Peer Remembers Jimmie Rodgers." Circa 1953
www.bluegrasswest.com.

Perry Ellis (advertisement). "Men's Fashion Spring 2005." *New York Times*,
March 13, 2005.

Peterson, Richard A. *Creating Country Music: Fabricating Authenticity.*
Chicago: University of Chicago Press, 1997.

Philips, Chuck. "Record Label Chorus: High Risk, Low Gain." *Los Angeles
Times*, May 31, 2001.

Porterfield, Nolan. "Hey, Hey, Tell 'Em 'Bout Us: Jimmie Rodgers Visits the
Carter Family." In Kingsbury, *Country: The Music and the Musicians*, 12–39.

Putman, Curly. "Green, Green Grass of Home." Sony/ATV d/b/a Tree Publishing Co.

Radio's Revolution and the World's Happiest Broadcasters. Directed by Richard Fatherley. Kansas City: Chapman Recording, 1998, radio documentary, www.reelradio.com.

"Rebels and Martyrs: The Image of the Artist in the Nineteenth Century." Press release, National Gallery (London), 2006.

Reynolds, Ed. "Nashville Confidential: A Country Music Songwriter Talks About His Biggest Hits." *Black and White*, May 3, 2007 www.bwcitypaper .com.

"Robbins, Hargus 'Pig.'" www.countryworks.com.

Robbins, Hargus "Pig." Country Music Hall of Fame presentation, notes by author, Nashville, TN. May 19, 2007.

Roethke, Theodore. "In a Dark Time." gawow.com/roethke/poems.

Rogers, Kenny, and Len Epand. *Making It with Music: Kenny Rogers' Guide to the Music Business.* New York: Harper and Row, 1978.

Rose, Mark. "George Jones: Last Exit Off a Dark Highway." *Village Voice*, September 23–29, 1981.

Rosen, Craig. "George Jones Pleads to DUI." *Yahoo! Music* www.music.calaunch .yahoo.com.

"Ryman Auditorium Hosts Ceremony to Announce Certification as National Historic Landmark." Press release, Ryman Auditorium June 22, 2001 www .ryman.com.

"The Ryman Chronology." www.ryman.com.

Sante, Luc. "Yodel, Escher, Bach." *Book Forum*, Fall 2001.

Schultz, Barbara. "George Jones' 'He Stopped Loving Her Today.'" *Mix*, July 1, 2001 mixonline.com.

Schuyler, Thom. "Sixteenth Avenue." Screen Gems-EMI Music, Inc.

Segal, David. "In New York, a Toast to Justice: Civil Rights Saga Edges 9/11 Commission Report at the National Book Awards." *Washington Post*, November 18, 2004.

Self, Philip. *Guitar Pull: Conversations with Country Music's Legendary Songwriters.* Nashville: Cyprus Moon Press, 2002.

Shell, Larry, and Larry Cordle. "Murder on Music Row." Sony/ATV d/b/a Tree Publishing Company.

Sherrill, Billy, and Curly Putman. "My Elusive Dreams." Sony/ATV d/b/a Tree Publishing Co.

"The Sherrill Sound." *Time*, October 22, 1973.

Sterling, Christopher H., and John Michael Kittross. *Stay Tuned: A History of American Broadcasting*, 3 ed. Mahwah, NJ: Lawrence Erlbaum, 2002.

Stewart, Karle. "The Reellife" www.thereellife.com/d.php.

"The Story Behind the Song: 'He Stopped Loving Her Today.'" National Music Publishers' Association. *News and Views* 6034 (Summer 2004) www.nmpa .org/pdf/newsletter/summer2004.pdf.

Strauss, Neil. "The Pop Life: David vs. Goliath to a Rock Beat." *New York Times*, October 3, 2002.

Susman, Gary. "'Fly' Girls." *EW.com*, June 18, 2002 www.ew.com.

Teachout, Terry. "Grand Ole Music." Review of *In the Country of Country* by Nicholas Dawidoff and *Three Chords and the Truth* by Laurence Leamer. *New York Times Book Review*, June 29, 1997.

Thomas, Kelly Devine. "The Selling of Jeff Koons." *Art News*, May 2005.

Thomas, Susan. "Music City's High Life." *Tennessean*, September 2, 1984.

Tianen, Dave. "Urban's Country More Than Credible." *Milwaukee Journal Sentinel*, June 6, 2004.

Tosches, Nick. *Country: The Twisted Roots of Rock 'n' Roll*. New York: Da Capo, 1985.

———. "Honky-Tonkin': Ernest Tubb, Hank Williams, and the Bartender's Muse." In Kingsbury, *Country: The Music and the Musicians*, 152–75.

———. *The Nick Tosches Reader*. New York: Da Capo, 2000.

———. *Where Dead Voices Gather*. Boston and New York: Little, Brown, 2001.

Trilling, Lionel. *Sincerity and Authenticity: The Charles Eliot Norton Lectures, 1969–1970*. Cambridge: Harvard University Press, 1972.

Tyrangiel, Josh. "The Dixie Chicks Get Serious." *Time*, August 19, 2002.

Wakin, Daniel J. "Schoenburg, Bach and Us." *New York Times*, March 27, 2005.

Whitburn, Joel. *Pop Hits: Singles and Albums: 1940–1954*. Menomonee Falls, WI: Record Research, 2002.

———. *Top Country Singles: 1944–2001*. Menomonee Falls, WI: Record Research, 2002.

———. *Top Pop Singles 1955–2002*. Menomonee Falls, WI: Record Research, 2003.

"Who Discovered Electricity?" www.wisegeek.com.

Williams, Hank Jr. "Blues Man." Bocephus Music.

Williams, Roger. "Hank the Great." In Carr, *The Illustrated History of Country Music*, 187–99.

Wilson, Charles Reagan. "Digging Up Bones: Death in Country Music." In McLaurin, Melton A., and Richard A. Peterson, eds., *You Wrote My Life: Lyrical Themes in Country Music*, 113–30. Philadelphia: Gordon and Breach, 1992.

Winter, Caroline. "Me Myself and I." *New York Times Magazine*, August 3, 2008.

Wolfe, Charles. "The Birth of an Industry." In Carr, *The Illustrated History of Country Music*, 30–72.

———. "The Legend that Peer Built: Reappraising the Bristol Sessions." In Kingsbury, Paul, ed., *The Country Reader: Twenty-five Years of The Journal of Country Music*, 3–20. Nashville and London: Country Music Foundation Press and Vanderbilt University Press, 1996.

———. "Modern Country." In Carr, *The Illustrated History of Country Music*, 277–339.

———. "The Triumph of the Hills. Country Radio 1920–50." In Kingsbury, *Country: The Music and the Musicians*, 40–63.

Wynette, Tammy (with Joan Dew). *Stand By Your Man*. New York: Simon and Schuster, 1979.

"You Shake My Nerves—The Jerry Lee Lewis Story." BBC Radio documentary. Excerpt transcripts. www.bbc.co.uk.

Young, J. R. "The Singing Cowboys." In Carr, *The Illustrated History of Country Music*, 138–63.

Zacharek, Stephanie. "Can Women Save Country Music?" *Salon*, September 14, 2002 www.salon.com.

Personal interviews and correspondence:

Booth, Alison. Email to Bobby Braddock, May 30, 2008.

———. Email to author, June 3, 2008.

———. Email to author, 11:48 a.m., June 13, 2008.

———. Email to author, 3:35 p.m., June 13, 2008.

Braddock, Bobby. Interview by author, audiotape, Nashville, TN, April 21, 2005.

———. Email to author, June 7, 2008.

———. Email to author, August 25, 2008.

———. Email to author, September 9, 2008.

Bradley, Lou. Interview by author, audiotape, Nashville, TN, April 20, 2005.

———. Interview by author, audiotape, Nashville, TN, June 19, 2008.

Butler, Larry. Interview by author, audiotape, Nashville, TN, December 28, 2004.

Carrigan, Jerry. Interview by author, audiotape, Nashville, TN, April 21, 2005.

Isenhour, Jack. Email to Alison Booth, June 3, 2008.

Jones, George. Interview by author, audiotape, Nashville, TN, January 25, 2007.

Kirkham, Millie. Interview by author, audiotape, Nashville, TN, March 22, 2005.

———. Interview by author, audiotape, Nashville, TN, March 23, 2005.

———. Interview by author, audiotape, Nashville, TN, March 25, 2005.

Mack, Reggie. Conversation with author at George Jones University, Franklin, TN, March 30, 2007.

McCoy, Charlie. Interview by author, audiotape, Nashville, TN, October 10, 2006.

Mitchell, Emily. Interview by author, audiotape, Nashville, TN, April 26, 2005.

Moore, Bob. Interview by author, audiotape, Franklin, TN, October 7, 2004.

———. Interview by author, audiotape, Nashville, TN, November 10, 2004.

———. Interview by author, audiotape, Franklin, TN, November 29, 2004.

———. Interview by author, audiotape, Nashville, TN, February 9, 2005.

———. Interview by author. Notes. Nashville, TN, February 9, 2005.

Olynick, Brent. E-mail to author, December 7, 2007.

Putman, Curly. Interview by author, audiotape, Nashville, TN, April 13, 2005.

Reynolds, Ron "Snake." Interview by author, audiotape, Nashville, TN, April 20, 2005.

———. Interview by author, audiotape, Nashville, TN, June 16, 2008.

Robbins, Hargus "Pig." Interview by author, audiotape, Nashville, TN, December 10, 2004.

Sherrill, Billy. Interview by author, audiotape, Nashville, TN, March 30, 2005.

———. Interview by author, audiotape, Nashville, TN, June 2, 2008.

Wade, Pete. Interview by author, audiotape, Nashville, TN, April 19, 2005.

———. Interview by author, audiotape, Nashville, TN, April 20, 2005.

———. Interview by author, notes, Nashville, TN, June 2008.

INDEX

CPSIA information can be obtained at www.ICGtesting.com
Printed in the USA
BVOW05s0627160814

362673BV00002B/2/P

9 781628 461664